FINDING JOY

A MOTHER'S JOURNEY
AFTER LOSING TWO SONS

Judy Snoddon

◆ FriesenPress

Suite 300 - 990 Fort St
Victoria, BC, Canada, V8V 3K2
www.friesenpress.com

ISBN
978-1-4602-7251-0 (Hardcover)
978-1-4602-7252-7 (Paperback)
978-1-4602-7253-4 (eBook)

1. Family & Relationships, Death, Grief, Bereavement

Distributed to the trade by The Ingram Book Company

How does one cope with the suicide of one child followed by the death from cancer of another? Somehow this amazing women has struggled and found joy in the wave of what would seem insurmountable grief. One can extrapolate from her experience myriad ways to deal with losses of any kind. A must-read.
Diana C. Aspin, Writer of *Ordinary Miracles* (Red Deer Press)

It is unthinkable for any parent to lose a child, but Judy Snoddon lost both of her very different sons in very different ways. Instead of succumbing to grief, step by step and plant by plant, she drew on the strength of her own roots rebuilt, to establish a new garden filled with memories, friends, love, beauty, travel and laughter. To her surprise: on the painful journey from the depths of loss and despair, Judy Snoddon found joy, healing and solace. Finding Joy, with its treasuring of family, friendship, and community, and its determination to rejoice in the light that shines through the darkness, is the story of that journey.
Andrea Knight, editor

We can suffer the most excruciating losses and travel through the deepest grief, come out on the other side, and find joy again. Judy's journey has shown us that it is possible. Her unshakeable desire to honour the lives of her two sons would not allow her to perish. How easy it would have been to be consumed by her grief. She would have been well-supported. But she chose a different path. She chose to feel her pain, her loss and to write this beautiful book of healing, love and the incredible resilience of the heart and soul. What a gift to the world. I will be forever grateful for Judy.
Yvonne Heath, Speaker and author of *Love Your Life to Death*

Judy's presence energized our "work family." The warmth of her persona was like a ray of sunshine on a cold dark winter morning. Whether engaging a mother with a critically sick child or a hypochondriac with a hangnail, she had an amazing ability to listen consistently, enthusiastically and thoughtfully and was able to connect meaningfully with everyone. So that in her darkest moments, following the loss of her sons, when most would have been unable to cope or function, she was able to reach out to our patients with support, empathy and action and through this altruistic philosophy of GIVING was not only able to survive but thrive and find JOY. Judy spent 25 years working in a Bracebridge family medical clinic. She was receptionist... social worker... nurse... mentor... comedienne and friend.

David Kent

TABLE OF CONTENTS

This book is dedicated to the two sons we lost tragically too early in life:
Mark Andrew Snoddon November 11, 1975 – August 08, 1998
Jason William Snoddon March 28, 1974 – June 22, 2007
It is also dedicated to all my wonderful friends and family, the people
who form our circle of support, who have given me a reason to continue.

Life isn't about waiting for the storm to pass...
It's about learning to dance in the rain.

VIVIAN GREENE

INTRODUCTION

My husband Bill and I lost our younger son Mark to suicide at the age of twenty-two.

His brother Jason died of lung cancer at age thirty-three. Writing this book has been a cathartic way for me to preserve their memory and, I hope, offer a little guiding light to others.

Mark and Jason had an influence on so many people, especially on me. They are still teaching me as I ponder the questions that have arisen during this writing. In the following pages, you will read about my feelings and thoughts while events unfolded in my journey to survive.

I have found that there **is** life after death: mine. I have not been a stranger to depression and know how hard it is to concentrate on reading long passages. I hope this collection of events will be an easy read for you, and provide a helping hand. I have learned many life lessons through gardening – maybe they will plant some seeds of hope and healing in your own garden of life. My memory garden, described near the end of the book, reflects the importance of personal history and how our past plays a role in developing who we become.

We all have our own unique journeys. Some are easier than others. The important choice is to never give up and keep moving forward. We must keep ourselves open to lessons we learn along the way.

Who knows? You too may find joy.

MARK

Mark's Life

In the early morning of August 8, 1998, my younger son, twenty-two-year-old Mark, took his own life. Part of me died with him. There is a stigma that comes with suicide. It is too often seen as the waste of a good life and what it could have been. It has taken me fifteen years to be able to say the word suicide without feeling a sharp pain that consumes my entire body with sadness, guilt and anguish. Why didn't I see it coming? I asked myself. Was I a bad parent? Where did I go wrong?

*****

Mark was born on November 11, 1975. It was Remembrance Day. There was a horrendous storm swirling around outside that caused a power outage.

During the previous few days, I had felt unwell with a virus. Since I was feeling achy and tired and the power was out, my husband Bill and I decided to go to bed early. All at once, I realized that I was experiencing a different kind of discomfort that was accompanied by a new pressing pain that seemed to come and go. Bill got a flashlight, and we started to time the cramps. Oh no! They weren't cramps; they were contractions, and they were coming five minutes apart. We phoned my Mom and Dad to come and stay with our nineteen-month-old son Jason. In the meantime, a neighbour came to stay until they arrived.

On the way to the hospital, Bill and I had to make our way around several fallen trees. My labour was starting much too early and I prayed that it was just a false alarm. As I was wheeled into the emergency department, the hospital's power also failed. I was about to say that I couldn't deliver a baby in the dark, when the emergency generator cut in.

Mark entered the world in the early hours of the morning. Before I could even hold my precious four-pound, eleven-ounce infant, he was immediately taken away so they could work on him. What should have been the most magical time of childbirth turned into a heart-wrenching time of fear and concern. The next time I set eyes on my little guy, he was hooked up to tubes and was gasping for every breath. I could tell he was a little fighter, but when they brought him over to my hospital bed to say goodbye, he looked so fragile. They wanted me to say goodbye before I even had time to say hello and show him a mother's love.

Mark was six weeks early; his lungs were underdeveloped, so he was rushed one hundred and twenty-five miles by ambulance to Sick Children's Hospital, in Toronto. I was weak and dehydrated and the doctors felt that I might still be contagious, so I had to stay anxiously behind in our local hospital. There were daily phone calls to monitor his progress, but I felt so helpless and out of touch.

Mark entered the world with a flurry of excitement and from that point on, we didn't have very many dull moments. As a matter of fact, he probably would have enjoyed the excitement of the ambulance ride to Sick Kids. I, on the other hand, would have preferred to keep him tucked safely in my arms.

Being a full-time mom, I had never been away from my older son, Jason, who was still a toddler. I needed the comfort of being near him, so my doctor agreed to discharge me earlier than planned. It was nice to be home, but my heart still ached for Mark. I decided to wash my hair, thinking that it would make me feel better. Washing it in the bathroom sink would allow me to keep Jason close; he could stand beside me on the toilet seat where he could watch me and we could chat. While I was washing my hair and we were talking, he was holding a small plastic baseball bat from Avon that was filled with aftershave lotion. All of a sudden, he bit into the bat and the top broke off. Before I could grab it, he gave me an impish look and quickly drank some of the aftershave. I couldn't believe it!

I didn't think he had ingested much, but I couldn't take the chance. I made a frantic call to my doctor's office. After they phoned the poison hotline, to be on the safe side we decided to take him to the hospital. The hospital staff gave Jason a drink to make him sick. When they couldn't get him to swallow it, I told them to just tell him that it was juice. He immediately gulped it down. The doctor decided to keep him overnight for observation.

So there we were, with both our babies in different hospitals. Bill and I were distraught. Fortunately, we were able to bring Jason home early the next morning. At least one of our children was back in the nest.

Mark was kept at Sick Kids Hospital in Toronto, on a continuous positive airway pressure (CPAP) machine for a few days, and then he was transferred to the Orillia hospital, which was closer for us. Bill and I were finally able to spend some precious moments holding our tiny new addition, bonding with him and showing him our love. A week later, he reached five pounds, and we could bring him home. Our little family was complete at last.

During his first three months, Mark spent a lot of time sleeping and catching up. It was during these months that I was blessed to witness the emergence of a wonderful little person. He was always smiling and had a loving, comical, determined personality. All those aspects remained part of his character as he grew up. I have so many memories of how loving and thoughtful he was. From the very beginning, our son taught us that, when he made his mind up, there was no changing it. He also became a daredevil who was never afraid to try something new. His brother Jason was the complete opposite in looks and personality. Jason was more of a dreamer and liked to talk about what he was going to do instead of carrying anything through. He was quite happy to watch Mark, in amazement, from the sidelines.

When Mark was about three, I heard Jason yell, "Mom! Come quick! Mark's going to ride his snow machine over the retaining wall!" That retaining wall was four feet high. I ran down the basement stairs to the patio door just in time to yell, "Mark, don't you dare do it." The next thing I saw was Mark flying through the air holding on tightly to his small red and black plastic snow machine. He made an almost perfect landing in the snow. Thank goodness he was wearing a thick snowmobile suit and a helmet. We used to say that Mark had an Angel on his shoulder.

That helmet came in handy another time, when Mark came in from playing and was too impatient to wait for me to remove the child-proof gate at the top of the basement stairs. When he started climbing over it, the gate gave way and Mark went tumbling backwards down to the bottom of the stairs. I was afraid of what I might find when I reached him. The carpeting on the stairs, the heavy snowsuit and the helmet saved him from another potential disaster.

There are so many memories of adventures – large and small, heart-stopping and hilarious – with my two boys. When they were about four and six, they proudly announced that they were going to perform a daring feat. Their plan was to jump off their playhouse – a fort on stilts that we had built for them – into the deep snow. As I watched them from the window, the two crusaders courageously waded through the snow and up the ladder to the playhouse balcony, proudly waving before Jay began his descent. He put one leg over the railing and, when that didn't feel right, tried the other leg. I think he tried the first leg one more time. While Jason was busy finding the right position, Mark just took the plunge. The next thing I saw was Jason climbing down the ladder to help his little brother who was stuck in the snow up to his waist. This time, it was Mom's turn to trudge to the rescue. When I lifted Mark out, his boots stayed in the snow. He had to lie on the snow, with his feet in the air, while I dug his boots out. He looked like a puppy waiting for a belly rub. Mark held his snow-filled boots, while I carried him back to the house. We all made it inside, safely, for a cup of hot chocolate. Jason never did get a chance to jump, and I still laugh every time I picture this comedy act.

When the boys were about seven and eight, my girlfriend Merle and I took them to Canada's Wonderland. All the way there, Jason bragged that he was going to ride the tallest roller coaster and, for once, Mark just listened. As soon as we arrived, Mark took off with excitement, while Jason grabbed my purse strap, yelling, "Mark! Wait up!"

We headed to the smallest roller coaster to start. Unfortunately, there was a mix-up in the lines and Jason ended up riding alone in the coaster, leaving us to wait for the next ride. After we finished, we discovered a pale, wide-eyed Jason standing frozen at the gate. His hair was all tousled, and his glasses were resting lop-sided on his nose.

"I thought I was going to die!" he exclaimed.

Mark, on the other hand, couldn't wait to go on the biggest loop-the-loop. The rest of us were not prepared to go on that ride, but there was no way I could discourage Mark. Finally, I told him he could go, but he would have to do it alone. When he started up the line, I thought he would be turned away because of his height, or he would lose his nerve. We all watched from the sidelines until we saw Mark getting in the front seat, by himself.

I held my breath. What if he tried to jump out, or got scared? Jason couldn't believe that Mark was going on his own, and ran to the exit, to meet his brother when he got off. Of course, Mark was thrilled with the ride.

One day, Bill discovered that Mark had been playing with matches in the basement. He gave him a stern lecture about how he could have burned the house down. Bill said if Mark liked starting fires so much, he could keep the woodstove lit in the basement.

A few months later, Bill gave up trying to get a brush pile to burn and went into the house. Mark stayed behind, determined to get the fire started. He wanted to be a hero to his Dad. Once he got it going, though, it really took off and Bill had to call the local fire department. It wasn't Mark's fault, but he felt so awful that he took his hatchet into the bush and chopped at a tree until his hands were blistered. He seemed to think that he had to punish himself and get rid of his frustrations at the same time. That worried me, but Mark never lost his fascination with fire and grew up to become a firefighter.

Mark never failed to amaze us. By the time he was about twelve, he was being picked on by some of the neighbourhood teenagers. One day, our doorbell rang and a couple of frantic teenage boys told us that they needed help. A friend of theirs had drunk a mickey of gin and was threatening to jump off a high cliff. Why they came to our door, I will never understand, because these were the very older boys who always gave Mark a hard time. But Mark didn't hesitate; he knew where the cliff was and ran off before we could stop him.

We told the other boys to get into the back of our truck and take us to their friend. We hadn't driven far when we saw Mark walking towards us with his arm around the boy. The boy was in bad shape. He kept saying, "What time is it? I'm late. My mom is going to be worried." Mark took off his new watch and placed it on the boy's arm, saying, "It's all right. You're fine. Now you won't have to worry about the time." We took the boy home and found out later that his mother had had to take him to the hospital for alcohol poisoning. That night, I told Mark how proud I was of him, especially for giving away the watch that he loved. Mark said, "Now I know why he picked on me. I guess he was really hurting."

All the same, Mark was certainly no angel. Well, maybe he was, but his halo was just a little tarnished. When he was about fifteen, we moved from Bracebridge to our dream home on Lake of Bays. I promised the boys that they wouldn't have to switch high schools. Since I had a job as a receptionist in a doctor's office in Bracebridge, I could drive them to school every day. Still, Mark and Jason hated being away from their friends and often had buddies over to spend the weekend. When they had friends over, I always tried to stay awake until I knew they were safely asleep, but they pulled the wool over my eyes one time. Mark and his partners-in-crime snuck outside and pushed my new car down the road, just out of hearing distance. Mark then took his friends on a thirty-mile joy ride to Bracebridge. They drove up and down the main street a couple of times and then came home. Anything could have happened. I didn't find out about this incident until years later when Mark decided to spill the beans.

Another time, Mark got into a fight after school. The next day, the police came to the school and took Mark to jail in handcuffs. There had been a lot of fighting at the school and the police wanted to make an example of him. I got the call at work that my son was in custody. I broke down in an empty office, but was soon needed back at my desk. The police officer told me that I could pick Mark up after work. Although he wasn't going to be held in custody, he would have to go on trial because he had been charged with an offence. Mark and I wrote a letter to the judge and got several other people to write character references for my son. At the time, I thought that there couldn't be anything worse than sitting in a court room watching my son on trial. Fortunately, he was only given community service.

I was so worried and upset about this incident that I had a conversation with one of the doctors I worked for, Dr. Kent, who had been one of Mark's cub-scout leaders. He assured me that Mark was a good kid and he would turn out fine. On the totem pole of life, he pointed out, this event was pretty low. I guess he was right.

My relationship with Mark had all the usual ups and downs of any mother-teenager relationship. One time, when Mark thought I was being unfair about something, he told me that he was leaving. I can still picture myself running down the highway after him, in my housecoat and pink fuzzy slippers, saying, "Mark, listen to reason. Let's talk about it. Don't forget I love you." He just kept taking those long-legged strides, putting distance between us, as he walked the ten miles to his friend's house in Baysville. Mark phoned to tell me that he had talked things over with his friend's father and now understood where I was coming from. "By the way," he asked, "could you pick me up for school tomorrow?"

"Yes of course I will," I said. "I'm just glad you're all right. Don't forget I love you."

There wasn't anything that Mark wasn't ready to try once the opportunity presented itself. At only fifteen-years-old, he got a special gun licence and shot a deer. His Grandfather, Papa, as Mark called him, who came from a pioneer family, was overjoyed. I can still picture Mark and Papa hugging each other and jumping up and down with excitement. Jason, on the other hand, was too sensitive to even think of killing an animal. He wanted nothing to do with hunting or guns.

The minute Mark turned sixteen he got his driver's licence. Jason was quite willing to wait until he was eighteen to take a driver's education course. In the end, they were both good drivers.

We also survived the normal hormonal teenage years, when tempers flared, parents knew nothing, and if you said, "Good morning," you were being critical. Miraculously, at about nineteen, a light bulb seemed to come on in Mark's head, and life made sense again.

*****

Mark's gentle, caring, side showed itself in so many ways. He loved his family, especially his Grandma and Papa and was always willing to lend a helping hand to whomever needed it. He was the type of kid who would help elderly people across the street, or carry their groceries just because it was a thoughtful thing to do. No matter what he did, he had the ability to win me over with his beaming smile and special hugs. He could light up a room with his smile and he was a kid magnet. He loved children and they loved him. He had tons of patience and knew how to entertain them with his sense of fun. He would have made a wonderful dad.

Mark's favourite time of year was Christmas. His excitement was contagious. He always made such a big deal over presents by either modeling them or demonstrating how they worked. Grandma and Papa never missed a Christmas get-together. They would arrive with a car load of gifts, food and treats. Jason and Mark seemed to bond over the holidays and got along exceptionally well during those times. We enjoyed family games, quality time, traditional family feasts, and always some guitar playing by Papa and Jason.

I remember one Christmas when Jason didn't come home until Christmas morning. Mark was pacing and couldn't wait for him to arrive – probably because the gift opening was put on hold until Jay came through the door. When he finally arrived, Mark ran out to greet him. But instead of coming in immediately, Mark started checking out Jason's vehicle.

Mark was always worried about Jason, especially his truck maintenance. He put some cement blocks in the back of Jason's old half-ton
truck to help with traction, started checking the tires, and worried
when his brother had had his last oil change. Mark was the mechanic of
the two. Maintenance repairs weren't high on Jason's to-do list.

I could write many stories about Mark's love, passion and kindness,
but my favourite story is about the time when his Aunt Alfreida was
dying of cancer. She was very special to him but he kept putting off
going to see her. When he finally did go, he asked her what she missed
doing most. She told him that she missed going for her favourite
Chinese dish at a restaurant in Orillia, a town thirty miles away from
her home. After their visit was over, Mark made a date to come back
the following week. Her homecare workers later told me how excited
Alfreida was that her Mark was coming. She asked them to help make
her look pretty. Mark was also dressed up and surprised her with her
favourite Chinese dish from her special restaurant. Mark spoon-fed
her, in his caring way and they had a wonderful time together. It meant
so much to Alfreida. Words cannot express how proud I was of my son
after I heard the story.

*****

Like Mark's Papa, he had the ability to fix things. Bill got him a job
at Scotty's Garage and Service Station in Baysville. He followed in his
Papa's footsteps and began as an apprentice mechanic. Mark fit right
in and became very close to Scotty and his wife. He worked very hard
to please and impress his boss. Scotty thought Mark had the talent to
make a living as a mechanic and he expected a lot of him.

In his spare time, Mark rebuilt and painted an old blue truck that
became his pride and joy. One day, after a disagreement with Scotty,
Mark loaded up his tools and sped away in "Old Blue". The truck still
wasn't completely reliable and no one knew where he had gone.

We didn't hear from him until he phoned us a couple of days later.
Mark told me that he had driven all the way to Thunder Bay where a

friend was attending university. He was fine, he said, and didn't want me to worry. On the way there, he had slept in the cab of his truck with his precious red box of tools on the seat beside him. He held a wrench in his arms for protection. When he arrived and found his friends, they smuggled him into the dorm. He even snuck into a couple of lectures. University was cool, he said. He asked me to let Scotty know he was okay, and would report for work Monday morning.

I often told Mark that he had to learn to count to ten and think, before he made these rash decisions. Nothing was too bad that we couldn't talk about it.

It was while he was working at the garage that Mark, still a teenager, became the youngest member of the local volunteer fire department. Being a firefighter was his true passion. He loved the excitement and was almost always the first on the scene. The other fireman soon named him "Backdraft," after the movie that Mark loved and had watched so many times.

Once, when I was driving home from work, I was stopped by some members of the fire department at an accident scene. Mark's firefighter buddies said that Mark was inside the smoldering car, retrieving something. Another time, I saw a burning building and, again, was stopped. This time they told me not to look – Mark was on the roof of the building with a chainsaw.

Mark was the first to arrive on the scene when a neighbour of ours was having a heart attack. He gave the man CPR, which saved his life. The family now gives a donation to the Baysville Fire Department instead of sending Christmas cards.

Mark was also the first to find a missing neighbour who was lost in the bush. He saw the man kneeling in a valley and rushed down to help him. Unfortunately, Mark couldn't save him. The man had passed away several hours before and his body had remained in a kneeling position. Mark helped carry the man out. His experiences as a volunteer firefighter were often hard on him. Because we lived in a cottage community that was a long way from a hospital, it was often too late for CPR to save people. Mark saw more and did more, by twenty years of age than many of us ever do in a lifetime. I sometimes wonder if it was too much for him, even though his greatest dream was to be a full-time firefighter.

*****

One day, while he was pumping gas, Mark noticed a pretty girl in the back seat of the van. He was instantly smitten, and gave her one of his irresistible smiles. It turned out that her name was Tee. As they playfully flirted with each other, a spark ignited between them. Tee was working in Baysville for the summer and, like Mark, was in Grade 12. They dated all summer and the romance continued when Tee went back to finish school in Owen Sound. When Tee graduated, she moved to Baysville to work for her Aunt. The next year, Mark and Tee announced that they were getting married. They were both only twenty, but they were determined.

The night before the wedding, all the boys in the wedding party and a couple of other boys spent the night. On the day of the wedding, they all got dressed at our house. I loved the excitement, and confusion, of having all the boys there. They were all so young. Thank goodness I had the good sense to buy five pairs of black socks. Goodness knows what they would have worn with their tuxes. Dirty, mismatched, or white tube socks, would be my guess.

Before the service, a very proud Grandma and Papa came to the house to give everyone their blessing and have a special moment with Mark and Jason. The wedding took place at Norway Point Church and everyone came back to our house for pictures and drinks, before the reception in Baysville. Mark and Tee were on top of the world.

The newlyweds rented a house in Baysville. Tee got a job at the local bar and Mark continued his apprenticeship until Scotty sold the garage and moved to Niagara-on-the-Lake. At that point, Mark and Tee both began working for Bracebridge Rental, which was owned by our family friend, Bruce. Once again, Mark bonded with his boss, Bruce and his family. Bruce took him under his wing and had great plans for him. They worked hard, but always found time to play hard together.

Meanwhile, Scotty was putting pressure on Mark to come to Niagara-on-the-Lake to work in a garage with him. Mark was torn and didn't want to let either of his mentors down. Finally after a lot of soul-searching, Mark and Tee moved to Niagara-on-the-Lake. Mark decided that he should finish his mechanic's apprenticeship, which he thought would be a better stepping-stone to a full-time position in a fire department. If a job in the fire department didn't work out, he figured, at least he would have a trade to fall back on. It all made perfect sense.

But something seemed wrong. Whenever Mark called, I noticed he was different. He seemed to be so stressed. He was working very hard trying to make a good impression on both Scotty and his new boss and he had never been away from home before. Tee was also working shifts in a winery restaurant and he missed the two of them spending their evenings together.

When Tee and Mark announced they were coming home to celebrate their second anniversary, I was over-the-moon with excitement. We had a party planned and had even rented a waterski boat for all their friends. The Thursday night before they arrived, I bought enough groceries for a small army and I was determined to get all of Mark's favourites. I told everybody I met in the grocery story that Mark and Tee were coming home.

Bill and I were already asleep when they finally arrived Thursday night. In true Mark form, on the way home, they couldn't resist stopping for a lengthy visit with their old boss, Bruce and his wife. I was just getting up Friday morning, when I heard a familiar voice.

"Mom, are you decent?"

Mark came bursting into my bedroom, wrapped his strong, caring arms around me, and told me how much he missed and loved me. My Mark was home and he made my day.

Mark, Tee and Bill made plans to spend Friday visiting friends in Barkway. I had to work. When I arrived home that evening, Mark and I spent some quality time together, and Tee and Bill went to bed. Mark wanted to reminisce about his childhood, which wasn't out of the norm for him. He seemed a bit restless and melancholy, but his spirits were good. He told me that he and Tee had found a house to rent, and proudly added that they had saved enough money for first and last month's rent. He was also excited about making some contacts with the Niagara Fire Department. We chatted for a while longer and then he insisted that he was going to visit his friends in Baysville. I begged him not to go because we had the big party planned for the next day and I was afraid he would be too tired. He made a few funny gestures and comments that made me laugh out loud, gave me a big, special hug and kiss, put one hand on the door, the other on his hip and with that great big wonderful smile, said; "M-o-t-h-e-r. Have I ever let you down before?"

"Y-e-s," I answered.

I spent a sleepless night, rolling and tossing, worrying and waiting, for Mark to arrive home. Finally, in the early hours of the morning, I was relieved to hear the car pull into the driveway. I heard Mark come up the stairs then go back down. When I heard the blast of the shotgun, I angrily ran down the stairs to see what the heck Mark was shooting at.

I was not prepared for what I found.

Only seconds after the gunshot rang out, I found myself standing over my young son's body.

Some say when the soul leaves, it hovers over its body. If that were true, Mark would have seen his heartbroken mother discovering that terrible, devastating scene.

SKETCH OF MARK BY DOROTHY HILLMAN

We were dazed and confused. There was no note left behind, no explanation. His friends from the night before offered few clues. They said Mark had been his old, jovial self. He had only had a couple of beers, they said. He had reminisced, and was excited about the party we had planned for the next day.

The entire community was in a state of shock. He was the least likely person to end his life this way.

I found myself on automatic pilot, making funeral plans and phone calls and going through the necessary motions. Close friends and family gathered around us to help us share our grief and bewilderment.

On the Sunday afternoon, Jason came home and was surrounded by a few friends who offered support. A bunch of Mark's friends showed up at the same time. We all sat in the family room, poring over photo albums, trying to find pictures to take to the funeral home. Looking through those old photo albums had been one of Mark's favourite pass-times. Now it seemed so bittersweet.

*****

One event that will always have a lasting impression on me was a special visitor who appeared the afternoon I was writing Mark's eulogy for the funeral. This eulogy was the very last gift I could give my son, and it had to be right.

I was lying on my bed, searching for the right words, searching for answers, trying to find a way to defend my son for taking his own life. I was feeling totally numb, alone, and heartbroken. Suddenly my daughter-in-law, Tee, came into the room and said, "Jude, you have to come and see this!"

We walked together down the hallway, to the glass door that led to the outside and saw a young buck deer standing in the yard. He seemed to be paying attention to the section of our yard that Mark had recently cleared and tilled for me. He looked up at us, as if giving approval for the beginnings of a garden. Then he strolled over to the small, white, lilac that Mark had so often clipped off when he was too hasty with the riding lawn mower. Amazingly, the lilac had survived, and was sprouting a few new green shoots. As the little buck sniffed the greenery, it must have tickled. His eyes began to sparkle as he once again peered up at us. His head was cocked to one side, as he twitched, and wiggled his nose in a way that made us laugh. It was just the type of humorous action that Mark had used so many times to lighten the moment. Tee and I stood with arms around each other, fixated on our visitor. Ever so slowly, he moved towards the edge of our property. He took one long, last look toward us, then gingerly made his way into the forest.

As we stood there, holding onto the moment and each other, we both felt that this visit was Mark's way of saying goodbye.

After that day, the little buck appeared every year on August 8, the anniversary of Mark's death.

*****

The next day was the visitation at the funeral home, and I was overwhelmed by the number of people who attended. At one point, the mourners were lined up around the block waiting to come in to express their sympathy. I planted myself beside the coffin and made sure that I thanked and hugged every person. It was important for me to show my appreciation. It gave me a sense of pride that Mark had an effect on so many different individuals. Most people said they were sorry. Others had stories they wanted to share.

A sorrow shared is a sorrow diminished.

UNKNOWN

One friend remembered Mark, standing on stage at the local bar, singing *I'm a Little Teapot* in a Donald Duck voice. That made me laugh. Only Mark could pull that one off. Another stranger told me about the time he pulled up to the gas pumps with a large U-Haul van loaded with furniture. As Mark started pumping the man's gas, he asked him where he was moving. The man told Mark that he had just purchased a cottage and had no idea how he was going to unload the furniture. Mark got directions to the cottage and told the man he would bring a couple of buddies over to help him unload his furniture in the morning. The new cottager didn't think Mark would ever show. But sure enough, right on schedule, Mark fulfilled his promise. Being from the city, the man was amazed. He made a point of coming to let me know what a great guy my son was.

A local couple and their son and daughter came in. Mark had spent a lot of time at their home and was treated like a member of the family. Their daughter and son had worked with him at the garage and they were devastated. The parents told me that their son had also joined the local fire department and had recently been unable to revive a drowning victim. The son was having trouble coping, so his family got in touch with Mark, in Niagara Falls. Mark was able to talk him through it and make him feel better. Now, two weeks later, the young volunteer had to deal with Mark's death. He was very emotional – Mark was like a brother to him. We all wondered how Mark had the ability to help someone else yet not be able to help himself.

A retired Etobicoke firefighter came through the line. I know that Mark had loved to listen to his stories. The firefighter had dusted off his old uniform to wear to honour Mark. After he gave me a hug, he took off his hat and placed it on the casket, saying that Mark deserved to borrow it.

One of the visitors who impressed me the most was one of Mark's friends who had been raised by a single mom. He had a lot of brothers and sisters from different fathers. I don't remember his father ever being in the picture. This boy, who came in looking handsome in a suit and tie, had had a hard upbringing, with little direction and few role models to follow. His eyes were filled with tears. After giving me his condolences, he gave me a hug. Then he moved toward the casket. He paused with sympathy, kissed his fingers and tenderly placed them by Mark's picture on the coffin. I was so touched by the gesture, I asked Mark's buddies if they could approach the young man to be an honorary pallbearer at the service the next day. He didn't disappoint me and won a special place in my heart. He was like a seed that fell by the wayside and became a beautiful flower, without the benefit of human touch, or influence.

Bill couldn't accept his son's death. He couldn't come near the coffin and stood outside trying to avoid people. He said if one more person said they were sorry, he would scream. He couldn't stand to listen to anyone talking about Mark. It hurt him too much to even say his name. He ended up missing so much. Jason tried to stand at the front beside me for a while, but couldn't handle it either. Poor Tee was lost; she was like a deer caught in the headlights. Her parents and my Mom and Dad sat with her at the front.

My own experience has taught me never to judge how people mourn. Everyone has to go through it in his, or her, own way. You never truly know how people are feeling inside.

I couldn't cry. I had to be strong for Mark and for everyone else. Some people express their grief with anger, and others, with silence. It seems to me that some people get over death quickly, while others never get over it. All you can do is try to understand. Listening to people talk about Mark gave me joy. Their hugs and condolences gave me strength. I couldn't stop talking about Mark because it kept him alive for me. When I thought about him and talked about him, he could still make me happy. The memories were all I had left.

I remember seeing the widow of Christopher Reeve – the actor who played Superman – talking about him shortly after his death. You could tell how much she loved and admired him, because when she spoke about him, she smiled in a way that made her glow. She felt the same way I did.

The night of the visitation was also Mark and Tee's second anniversary. They had planned to celebrate their anniversary by popping a bottle of champagne on the steps of the church where they made their wedding vows. After the visitation, it was important to Tee that both families, including Scotty and his wife, go to the church to drink a toast to Mark. It was a very emotional time for all of us. We were not only feeling the loss of Mark but also the loss of his marriage to Tee. We had such high hopes for their future.

The little white Norway Point Church sits in a picturesque setting, nestled among some towering red pines, on a point of land looking over Lake of Bays. As we stood there, on that brilliant moonlit night, we were comforted by the sound of a loon in the distance as the waves lapped against the shore in a consoling rhythm. The large pines encircled us, like old friends, as they gently swayed in the peaceful breeze. We tapped our glasses together and I made a toast to Mark and Tee's everlasting love. Everyone stood in silence, wondering what to do next. Just then, ever so slowly, the clouds began to gently roll across the moon, like a loving parent tucking us in. That was our cue to say good night.

*****

The next day, at the funeral, we were able to give Mark a special send-off. It was important to Tee to give him a firefighter's service. We walked behind the pumper truck from the funeral home to the church. The church was bursting at the seams, standing-room only. Several local fire departments attended and my cousin, Eric Taverner, a fire captain in Richmond Hill, brought some of his men in full uniform. Mark would have been thrilled beyond words.

I got through my eulogy about Mark. I called it "The Power of Love". In it, I expressed my thoughts that while love is wonderful, it can also be a burden. When a person loves the way Mark loved and tried to please everyone, it could be unbearable.

During the service, I found myself touched by how much love and energy I felt in the church.

Tee spoke next. In a tiny, low voice, she spoke about the little buck deer and how she knew it was Mark's way of saying goodbye. She told Mark how much she loved him. I don't think many people heard her, but I'm sure Mark did, and that was all that counted.

Mark's boss, Scotty, told the gathering that Mark was like a son to him. When he came to work the first day, Mark wore a brand-new white T-shirt. His first job was to tear the engine out of an old Volkswagen van. Mark wanted to prove himself and wouldn't give up. Scotty said that there wasn't much white showing on the shirt at the end of the day.

The Archdekin Medical Clinic, where I worked, was closed so that everyone could attend. It meant a lot to have my second family there. Two of the doctors made a point of coming over to me, right after the service, to give me a hug. They said that they couldn't stay for the reception but wanted me to know they would be thinking of me. A few weeks later, I learned that they had been camping with a group on an island in Georgian Bay. They hired a water taxi to take them to shore so that they could drive to attend the funeral and then drive back to meet the water taxi which took them back to join the other campers. It was evening before they got back to the island. Feeling melancholy and humbled by the fragility of life, they decided to spend some time out in their canoe alone. They both had children Mark's age. They also wondered why bad things happen to good people. When I heard this story, I felt honoured that they cared enough to make such a special effort.

We were drained by the time we got home that night. I left everyone sitting around the kitchen table and went to lie on the couch in the family room. Tee came in and placed Mark's picture on the fireplace mantel so I could look at it while I rested. I must have dozed off into a silly restless dream and woke up laughing to myself. My weary eyes fixed on Mark's picture and I was too quickly brought back to reality. A feeling of emptiness consumed me as I slowly let my heavy eyes fall shut once more. The next moment, I felt a gentle heavenly kiss caress my cheek. I will treasure that kiss, and that moment, for the rest of my life. My son had kissed me goodbye.

*****

A couple of days after the funeral, I decided to check out the bag we had brought home from the funeral home. Inside, along with the guest book and blank thank-you cards, I found a white sealed envelope addressed to me. Curious, I opened it up, to find a card with a picture of a mother deer with two little spotted fawns. Inside, there was a nice note from a patient from the clinic. I was really touched by the significance of the card – there is no way this lady could have known about our special little buck's visit, and how spiritual it felt to us. It was such a wonderful coincidence that I immediately called the lady to let her know how much the card meant to me and why. She told me that she was from Sweden where people told her that she had a gift of special intuitiveness. She didn't like sympathy cards and knew she should purchase this particular note card.

This was, definitely, a case of synchronicity – two events happening at the same time for a reason.

*****

A few days after the funeral, the old Volkswagen van that Mark had worked on his first day at Scotty's Garage and Service Station pulled into the driveway. The driver seemed to suit the old van. He had long hair and a beard and was considered the neighbourhood hippy. His grandparents, parents, and aunts had property on Lake of Bays; he had moved up from the States years before to reside there. Because the family cottages weren't winterized, he had built himself a garage with permanent living quarters up above it.

The man hesitated before getting out of the van. He started walking slowly up the driveway. I went out to greet him. With tears in his eyes, he apologized for not coming to the funeral. He said he couldn't handle funerals, but heard that his Volkswagen van had been mentioned.

Knowing the awful thing that happened outside our back door, he said, he couldn't understand how we could stay living in the house. He said that he had a vacant cottage and with a little work, we could move in there until we found a better place. I gave him a hug and said that there were a lot of memories in our old house, good memories that outweighed the bad. It was our home and we knew that Mark wouldn't want us to move. I thanked him and told him it was a very kind and generous offer.

I asked him to join me on a walk down to the dock and as we walked, we talked about Mark. Since he missed the funeral, I described how moving it had been and how proud Mark would have been. I also told him about the little buck deer and a few of our special stories. By the time we walked back, he understood more about why we wanted to stay. Having had a chance to talk about what a great guy Mark was made us both feel better. This neighbour will always be my Good Samaritan.

Seeking Solace

I had to escape and spend some time by myself. That day, the sunset was about to appear over Bigwin Island so I decided to take the canoe out to appreciate the moment. A solitary loon kept me company as I slowly paddled across the calm water. I watched, in awe, while the sky turned a brilliant crimson, complemented by swooping brush strokes of mauves and dove greys. Streaks of pale yellow and burnt orange added to this amazing masterpiece. Like rolling waves, the colours of the sky constantly changed. As a kind of finale, the majestic golden sun took centre stage and made the final curtain call as it slowly disappeared behind the island.

Mother Nature had dimmed her lights and wrapped me in the peaceful stillness of dusk. As the waves rocked my canoe, I felt consoled and finally allowed my grief to wash over me. I sobbed for the loss of my son. At last, I had found some solace and lingered in my new-found peace. It was almost dark before I walked up the path to the house. My respite was over.

A couple of days later, my dear friend, who I'll call BF, came to spend some quality time. He asked how I was feeling. I thought about the question and remembered a vision that came to me the night before. I saw myself walking down a long softly lit corridor with several doorways on both sides. I could see a glowing brighter light in the distance. The hallway was suspended in space. It wasn't scary; instead it felt mystical, calm, and safe. As long as I kept walking towards the light and didn't go through one of the doorways, I felt I would be fine. At the same time, I had the feeling that if I took a step through one of the doorways, I would fall into eternity, and be lost forever.

My friend wondered if the white hallway represented my need to stay in control. That made sense to me. As long as I stayed in control, in the hallway, I felt safe. The fact that the hallway was suspended in space must have represented the loss of Mark and the void it made in my life. The vision told me to keep walking straight ahead, one foot in front of the other, to rely on myself and on what was familiar. Making any rational decisions or plans at that time would be impossible. If I gave in to my grief and pain, and opened that doorway, I felt I would fall into an abyss.

Months later, I was watching a television program and I perked up when I heard someone talking about rooms and doorways. He explained that some people are stuck in rooms that could represent a bad marriage, an addiction, a poor job, a lack of self-esteem, being overweight, or feeling depressed. Every room, he said, has an unlocked door, but it takes a tremendous amount of courage to open the door and enter the next room. There is no way of knowing with any certainty whether the new room would be a better place, or a worse place. The important thing was to have enough strength to make the decision to try a new beginning. There would always be another doorway, or another room, that might be the right fit.

It is my belief that we must never give up until we find the room that allows us to be in the best place we can be. As we build our confidence, changing rooms becomes a lot easier. The next room could represent leaving the marriage, going for counseling, finding willpower, going to rehab, or asking a doctor for help. It might just mean something as simple as getting up in the morning and looking forward to a new day. If we are honest with ourselves, we all know what our rooms represent.

During my mourning period, my room was limited to a hallway.

After BF and I talked about my vision, we decided to take the canoe over to Bigwin Island. It was a fair distance and I wanted him to give me some paddling pointers in hopes of giving me something positive to think about. The water always had a way of soothing my soul. As we paddled, the sun glistened on the lake, creating sparkling diamonds all around us. By the time we made it to Bigwin, however, the weather was beginning to change. Dark grey clouds were rolling in, and we heard the sound of rumbling thunder in the distance.

Knowing how quickly bad weather could roll in on Lake of Bays, we immediately started back towards shore. About halfway back, it began to rain; thunder boomed and lightning flashed around us. I began to panic and paddled furiously for safety. Suddenly, we heard a deafeningly loud crack of thunder; a bolt of lightning seemed to strike right behind us. I screamed. Without thinking, almost by reflex, I pitched my paddle about ten feet out into the water.

"I can't believe you did that," a voice behind me said.

"I was scared out of my mind," I answered guiltily.

BF maneuvered the canoe to where I could retrieve my abandoned paddle. I worked with it until we safely reached shore. When we got there, I felt like kissing the ground. As we pulled the canoe onto dry land, my two neighbours came running down to see if we were safe. They had been watching from shore and saw a lightning bolt hit the water directly behind us. I confessed that I had tossed my paddle. So much for my peaceful canoe ride!

In retrospect I can say that the whole experience took my mind off my grief, if only for a short time. And it made for a terrific story.

A few months later, BF asked me if I was still walking down my white hallway. I told him that I thought so, but I felt I could go through any door, and still retain my footing. My hallway was finally on solid ground.

*****

Each one of the many sympathy cards we received after Mark died had a special meaning. It amazed me how some people had the ability to compose such touching words. One of the cards, the one that had the most meaning for me, didn't have any words at all. My friend BF had been struggling to find the right words – words that suited the card, and his feelings. One day, he just handed me the empty card, along with an apology. The photograph on the front of the card showed a small, colourful maple seedling growing out of a dark, bleak, rock surface. The little tree had managed to root itself and grow against all odds. I understood what BF was telling me: no matter how empty and hopeless my life seemed, I must not give up. If the little maple could survive, maybe I could as well.

I have learned from experience that the greater part of our happiness or misery depends on our dispositions and not on our circumstances.

MARTHA WASHINGTON

The New Normal

We were all trying to adjust to our new reality, stumbling through grief, in our own ways. We needed to stay close for the security and comfort of each other's existence to somehow fill the void that Mark had left, and at the same time try to make sense of the curve ball that life had thrown us.

Jason moved home for a year, saying that his plan was to heal us. He was having trouble dealing with the loss of his brother. He thought that Mark's death was easier for me because I had faith and believed that there was an existence after death. I also felt that things happened for a reason and we would all understand some day.

Jason felt that death was The End. He couldn't reconcile himself to the fact that someone who was so full of life could just be gone. Jason thought that Mark would accomplish everything for him. After all, he was already married and would give us grandchildren to carry on the family. To Jason, that would take the pressure off, because he wasn't ready and didn't know if he would ever be ready. I tried to assure him that it didn't matter. I just wanted him to be happy with whatever choices he made in life.

My boys loved each other, but they didn't have a lot in common, except their strong-willed personalities and their love of family. I didn't realize how deep Jason's feelings ran for his brother until he came home, on Mark's birthday, with a tattoo. Placed over his heart were the words: *November 11, 1975 – August 8, 1998.*

Tee had stayed with us after the fateful weekend of Mark's death. We had her things moved back from Niagara Falls and she got a job in Bracebridge. I was very concerned about her because she held her feelings inside. One night, I got up and noticed she wasn't in her bed. I panicked when I saw pillows pulled under the covers. I thought she had placed them there so we would think she was sleeping. Frantically, I ran down stairs, searching for her. I found her sitting in the family room, crying. When I told her how scared I was when I saw the pillows, she told me that she always slept like that so it would seem as if Mark was beside her.

It was one of the rare times we talked about our feelings. Tee, Jason, and I were all suffering in our own ways, but we all tried to put on brave fronts to hide our emotions and to protect each other and Bill. That's what families seem to do. We were in survival mode. It is often much easier to share grief with friends or acquaintances, rather than with close family.

I went back to work very soon after we lost Mark. I needed some purpose and stability in my life. While the doctors were healing others, I was mending myself. I felt empathy for the patients and when I was helping them, it made me feel better. It was very busy and fortunately it was too busy to think. The other women in the office would get annoyed at things that didn't seem to bother me. Everything seemed so minor compared to losing Mark.

Sometimes in the midst of chaos, routine keeps us sane.

UNKNOWN

It was strange. My desk area and phone at work seemed to be my control centre. I could function behind my desk, but if I moved away from it, I couldn't even finish a sentence. I couldn't remember words and talked in circles. I thought I was putting on a good show, but anyone who really knew me saw through it. I needed the job because

I loved what I did; it gave me some dignity and structure. We also needed the money because things were tight.

The girls and the doctors at work were very supportive. Work became my sanctuary as well as my escape. Unfortunately, I would work hard until my day off and then have trouble getting off the couch.

This puzzled me. How could I work so hard at work, yet when I came home, I couldn't find enough strength to move? At work, I was doing things for everyone else – it made me feel better at the time – but it also totally drained my extra strength. By the time I got home, the reality of my life set in. Every night, I would drive the thirty minutes home to find Bill, at the end of the kitchen table, with a beer in his hand. He would moan about the bad day he always had; there were very few nights he didn't ask, "Why?"

Angels on Duty

Tee told us that she needed some time away so she went to Baysville to spend some time with friends. At some point that evening, she phoned to tell us she was finishing a game of pool and then would come home.

She never returned.

I stayed awake most of the night, but told myself that no news must be good news. Perhaps she had decided to spend the night with friends. With still no word, the next day, I went to work feeling very unsettled. Around 10 a.m., Tee's boss, who was also a good friend, walked into the office and came right over to my desk. I must have turned white but before I could say anything, he said, "She's okay, but there's been a car accident."

On the way home from Baysville, Tee had lost control of her car. Perhaps she fell asleep from exhaustion. At any rate, she went through a set of guard rails and down a large embankment, into some rocks. The only thing she remembered was climbing up the embankment and walking to the house of some friends for help. The car was demolished. No one knew how she managed to get out alive. Tee was in shock, but miraculously only sustained a few bruises. She didn't want me to know, or to see the car, so she made arrangements to have it towed away. She was trying to protect me from any more hurt.

A week later, while we were cutting wood behind the house, an OPP officer came walking into the bush towards us. He handed me a wallet, and asked if I knew whose it was.

"Oh my God," I said.

There was Mark's firefighter's badge inside the wallet.

"That's my son's wallet. He passed away. How did you get it?"

The officer said that some people found it while walking near an accident site. Did I know anything about why it might have been there? I told him that he would have to talk to my daughter-in-law. Tee told him what had happened, but she refused to give the names of the friends who had helped her. They charged her with leaving the scene and made her pay for the guard rails. The police let her off lightly because they knew what we all had recently gone through. But poor Tee. She couldn't put the accident repairs through her insurance and lost her car.

I believe the fact that Tee survived with only bruises and Mark's wallet showed up were signs that Tee had an angel with her that night. Tee would prefer to believe she lived because she was wearing a seatbelt.

A Fatal Accident

About the same time we lost Mark, our community was shattered by news of a fatal car accident which involved an amazing young woman whom everyone admired. The girl's father made a point of coming to me with the story of his daughter's death. He knew that I would understand; he thought it might help me to share his grief.

Londa was an angelic, popular and determined person. She followed in her father's footsteps to become a teacher. Everyone knew that she and her husband had a wonderful future ahead of them.

One treacherous, snowy and icy night, Londa lost control of her vehicle and slid sideways into the opposite lane. She was struck by an oncoming car and then both cars were hit by another vehicle. One of the first vehicles on the scene was a mother and her sixteen-year-old son. The boy had just obtained his driver's licence that same day. When they approached Londa's car to see if they could assist, they saw Londa lying across the front seat. She was unconscious, but didn't seem in distress. A young man was kneeling beside her, comforting her and tucking her in a warm, yellow blanket. Once they realized everyone was being taken care of, they went on their way.

This story later came to the attention of Londa's parents. The person who told them hoped that it would bring them some peace to know that she hadn't suffered. Her Dad was confused. He had seen the wrecked car and knew that there was no way that anyone could have fit inside the vehicle beside her. There was no yellow blanket found at the crash scene. The accident had taken place in an isolated part of the highway. There were no homes in the area, no tracks leading to the accident site.

As Londa's father thought about the story, he recalled that Londa always had a bright yellow blankie as an infant. She and the blanket were inseparable. When he remembered this, his face lit up with a knowing smile of faith. He realized that this was one of life's mysterious miracles. On that cold winter evening, an Angel had taken care of his baby girl.

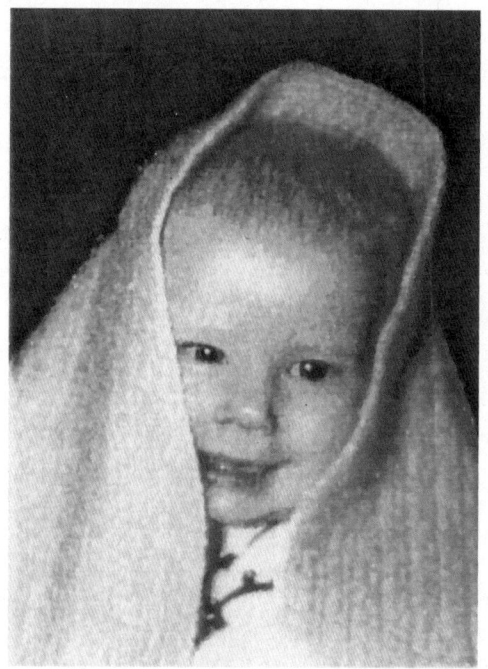

A Psychic Meeting

My girlfriend Pam, who lives in England, always seemed to have a psychic ability. But to her, it was more of a burden than a gift. I never took her ability very seriously. I didn't disbelieve it; I was just a bit skeptical.

Pam and I hadn't been in contact for a long time, In July 1998, she phoned me, out of the blue, to tell me that a life-changing event would happen to me, in August. The feeling was so strong, she said, that she had to call to let me know. I made a joke of it.

"Maybe I'm going to win the lotto or something." I said.

I asked if she thought the event was going to be something good. She said that she wasn't sure, but probably. A few weeks after we lost Mark, in August that same year, I remembered my conversation with Pam. I called her to let her know that she was right; my life would never be the same again. Pam felt terrible, and thought that she might have read it wrong because she cared too much for me. She swore that she would never give another person a message like that again.

A few months after Mark's death, as I was searching for answers, I heard about a psychic who was supposed to be very good. Her services were often used by the police to find missing bodies. What did I have to lose? I thought. I made an appointment, but I kept it a secret because I knew that Bill and my parents would think I was crazy. I knew that I was just searching for some insight into what had happened, during those missing hours between the time Mark left the house that night, and his return. What could have been so bad that he took his own life?

The psychic told me to bring one of Mark's personal items as well as a picture. I took Mark's shoes – the ones which were still sitting by the back door because I hadn't had the heart to get rid of them. I thought that since he had walked in those shoes that night, maybe they held some answers. Along with Mark's picture, I also took a picture of Jason to test her.

We met in my car in a vacant park. She took Mark's shoes and as she held them, we noticed that they seemed to get quite hot. All that she could tell me was that she felt he spent a long time by the water, thinking.

"What a character he must have been," she said, looking at Mark's picture.

She told me that she didn't feel that this was the first time that Mark had been on the Earth. In a past life, he had been a clown. I was amazed by this, because until Mark was about five, he had always said that he wanted to be a clown when he grew up. Later, he was the class clown and loved to imitate people and make people laugh. He was so fascinated by clowns that I was going to start a collection of clowns for him. When he got a caricature done at Ontario Place, and the artist asked what he wanted to be drawn as, the answer, of course, was as a clown.

The psychic really had no answers for me about Mark's decision to take his own life, but our meeting still made me feel better. If Mark had lived before, then there was hope that his spirit could come back and live again. She did look at Jason's picture and said that he could also tell some wild stories. She told me not to underestimate him. He was going to make me proud someday. She was totally right.

Real Sisters Listen with Their Hearts

There were times when I would talk my friend Sal's ear off for hours. She was more than a dear friend; she was a sister. Sal listened, patiently, while I talked about the boys, or about my latest miracle, or as I complained about Bill, and so on and so on.

"I can't even imagine, Jude," she would always say.

There may have been a little voice inside her yelling, "Would you just shut the hell up," but if there was, she never let me know. Instead, she would tease me to make light of the situation. We would end up laughing uncontrollably. That is a real friend. She kept me real. She could bring the best out in me at times when I lacked self-confidence, and couldn't see it in myself.

Sal and I first met in 1989, when we both started working at the Archdekin Clinic. She was on switchboard, and her sister Cathy was our office nurse. The three of us immediately connected and an amazing friendship blossomed. I was an only child, so when Sally and Cathy and their three sisters included me as a "sister," it was my saving grace. We had wonderful sisters' weekends with maybe a bit too much to drink – well, maybe just a tad. We would laugh until we cried one minute, and then solve the problems of the world the next. We had sisters' vacations, sisters' Christmas parties, sisters' shopping trips, and sisters' date nights.

Sally, Cathy and their sisters came from a wonderful family of eight. Their mother, Thelma, was the matriarch of the family and a real lady. She often shared our weekends until she died of cancer. I had the privilege of being included in the circle of sisters who gathered around Thelma's hospital bed when she passed away.

These women are born leaders and are very competitive. That was always great for me because I was happy to follow along and plug into their boundless energy. When I'm with them, I feel revitalized and there is never a dull moment. We love to tell the same stories, over and over, and always laugh as if it were the first time we'd heard them. One story we often tell is about the time we visited another sister, Val, in Scarborough, where she lives in a co-op apartment complex. While we were carrying in our suitcases and supplies for the weekend, I trailed behind with Thelma, carrying my sleeping bag, overnight bag, my purse and a bag of groceries. Mark hadn't been gone that long, so I shared with Thelma that I planned to be incognito that weekend. Just then, my foot caught in one of my bags and I fell noisily down five steps to the bottom of the landing. Almost immediately, two apartment doors opened simultaneously and the residents asked if everything was all right. I told them that I was fine because the sleeping bag had cushioned my fall. By then, the sisters were back on the scene killing themselves, laughing. So much for my incognito weekend!

It is never a complete sisters' weekend without going to a couple of Value Village stores looking for treasures and experiencing the thrill of the great find. Just imagine all of us standing outside the change room, with shopping carts, full of possibilities. There is nothing more fun than everyone trying on something and getting reactions from the rest of the group. Val and I are quite conservative, while Cathy and Sal are usually far out, weird, or wonderful. Nancy and Linda are somewhere in the middle.

At one point during each sisters' weekend, we could be heard singing the Supremes, or some other oldies. During our philosophical moments, Sal usually shares something she has learned from her hero Oprah. But in true Sal form, before the weekend is over, she always ends up as a comedy act singing some old rude song with a napkin, or something, on her head. These moments are always followed by roars of hysteric laughter, and Val saying, "You silly buggers." Laughter, girl talk, music and the company of my adopted sisters – this is the best medicine anyone could have.

Each one of my sisters has had her share of hard times, child-raising worries, and difficulties. But together, we have made life easier to bear. We've all come out the other side as stronger individuals. I raise a glass to my sisters.

Norway Point Church

Norway Point Church played an important role in my recovery. It's a feel-good church, situated in a restful setting, looking over the beautiful Lake of Bays. By the water's edge, there is a stone bench donated in memory of a mother. This is a perfect place to rest and find solace. There is an old bell on a stone base in front of the church that tolls to call everyone to worship. The church itself is painted pure white with a steeple and red roof. The simple, single-pane windows come to a point at the top; it resembles praying hands. You don't need fancy stained-glass windows at Norway Point Church, because when you look out, you see God's natural scenery. When we open the windows during a service, the leaves gently sway in the breeze and birds can be heard adding their melody to the hymns. Inside, the church is finished very simply, with natural wood walls and open rafters. Plaques representing past members have been lovingly placed between the two-by-four walls. There is also an impressive carved wooden altar at the front, with two matching carved chairs, that were donated by local Mohawk singer Os Ke Non Ton in memory of a friend, Lenore Kennedy, who had heard him singing while he weaved baskets by his teepee on the shore. She helped him become a world-famous singer who performed at the Toronto Exhibition as well as at the Royal Albert Hall in front of Queen Mary.

This simple church is a far cry from the many cathedrals that adorn Europe, but I felt closer to God here than in any of those masterpieces.

To me, cathedrals are just a celebration of man's workmanship; they are almost a type of idol. They are wonderful in their own way, but I can't help but feel how many children could be fed for the money it costs to construct them. That may, upon reflection, seem too harsh a statement. After all, the artists were creating masterpieces and works of art that are designed to be timeless and provide a place for generations of people to celebrate their love for and faith in God.

All denominations are welcome at this little church, and every Sunday a different minister brings a message. Sometimes I would bring flower arrangements for Sunday services. It gave me a purpose and I enjoyed sharing my flowers with the congregation. My Grandmother used to bring arrangements to her little country church and it made me feel good to continue the tradition.

Norway Point Church is a summer cottage church. On Sunday mornings, cottagers may come by boat, or walk along the path that follows the shore, under the towering red pines, dressed in relaxed summer attire that suits the atmosphere. When I drove to church, I also saw cottagers walking from the other direction, along the lake road that connects all the Glenmount cottages. Some members of the congregation would be waiting outside to accept my flowers, with appreciation, while they greeted everyone as they arrived. The church has a wonderfully welcoming and friendly atmosphere.

Inside, I was always filled with a feeling of peace and contentment, which was especially important to me after I lost Mark. When we "Passed the Peace," it was like old-home week. Everyone greeted each other with such joy that it gave me a sense of fellowship and belonging. How could one not love the following call to worship?

> As a loon calls over the water for its mate, so too does
> God call us to this place.
> As the sun which warms the flowers to bloom, so too does
> God's love encourage our growth.
> Like the rain nourishes parched land, Christ's word
> quenches our thirsty lives.

Like the rush of wind through majestic pines, God's spirit lifts and renews. Come Holy Spirit, help us to stand again as we worship with thanksgiving.

The year that Mark died, another member of the church decided to have a Christmas Eve service in memory of her friend. This gave me a sense of purpose. Mark and Tee were married there and because Mark loved Christmas so much, I donated all the decorations except the tree. Decorating the tree and decking out our little church got me through the first year.

Around the rafters, Bill and I strung white twinkle lights among greenery and poinsettias. When we were finished, they looked like stars shining from above. There were candles in mason jars, tucked in amongst pine cones and greenery, on the window sills. The altar was adorned with more greenery, white poinsettias and lights. The tree followed the same theme adorned with white doves and white and gold poinsettias. It was a wonderful place to spend my first Christmas Eve and to honour Mark.

I haven't been back to Norway Point Church since we moved from Lake of Bays, but I have fond memories and know that it provided an important stepping stone in my journey to healing.

Mark's Easter Visit

We spent the Easter following Mark's death at my Mom and Dad's. Tee brought her Mom, and Jason came alone. It was a family tradition that Mom cooked Easter dinner while I looked after Christmas and Thanksgiving. But that year was different. A task that other years just seemed to flow so easily, seemed to be too hard for Mom. Her nerves were frayed. Dad was trying to be his jovial self. He was always a good host and tried hard to make everyone feel welcome and comfortable. That day it wasn't easy; we could all feel a lot of tension in the room. Mark's death was taking its toll on everyone. Bill was a mess, drinking and crying, as usual. By now, his constant gloom and doom was getting to me. I knew that Mark would have been upset; he wouldn't want to be remembered that way. I felt Bill was spoiling Mark's memory, something that I was desperately trying to keep precious.

I was in the kitchen helping Mom when she asked me to get the napkins for the table out of the drawer in the dining room.

"If I were a napkin, where would Mom put me?" I asked myself trying to lighten the mood. I found the napkins, after looking through a couple of drawers. As I turned around to put them on the table...to my amazement...standing in the corner of the dining room...comfortably learning against the wall with a large, glowing smile...was...my Mark. Our eyes connected, for a moment and then he was gone. I felt all my tension lift.

I didn't want to spoil it by telling anyone; I wanted to wrap myself in the moment of it. I felt blessed, privileged.

During supper, while everyone else was still very uneasy, I just sat there with a smile on my face and kept staring at the empty corner. He looked so perfect and natural, not like the last time I had seen him.

A few months later, I shared this story with a father who had lost his son to suicide. I was hoping it would make him feel better knowing that his son's death wasn't necessarily the end. To my surprise, he got very angry with me. He was still suffering and was very bitter. He said that I had just *imagined* Mark. If my story were true, he asked, why hadn't his son's spirit visited him? I didn't have an answer for him. I gave all of this a great deal of thought and still firmly believe that I didn't just imagine Mark. He was there. Knowing how determined Mark could be, I think that he had unfinished business; he regretted what he had done. Perhaps he realized that he wasn't ready to go. My connection with him was especially strong because I was the one who found him. The other parent's child had been living in another city. The parents weren't there at the instant he passed away. Maybe he was ready to go on. Who knows? Ours is not to wonder why, just to be grateful and accept any blessings we receive.

You don't have a soul,
You are a soul,
You have a body.

C.S.LEWIS

A Letter from Mark

A couple of years after his passing, Mark made his presence known once more. Out of the blue, my friend Marg, whom I hadn't seen since Mark's funeral, phoned to let me know that she wanted to visit. She used to live next door to my parents and Mom thought of her as a second daughter. I invited her for lunch, suggesting that she come to my exercise class at the lodge next door. The class was held right before lunch so we could have more time for a visit. She agreed, and soon arrived, dressed in her workout clothing.

After lunch, we sat on the veranda and started to catch up. Marg seemed to be a little nervous, as if there was something on her mind. I asked if she was all right. She said there was something that had taken her six months to build up the courage to tell me. She was afraid that I would think she was crazy. I reassured her that I had a very open mind, especially since losing Mark. Encouraged, she explained that she had been taking meditation classes and had attended a whole-day session in which no one was allowed to speak. Soft music played in the background. *In the Arms of the Angels* by Sarah McLachlan was playing when Mark came to her. She said she had never experienced anything like it. She silently argued with him, begging him to bother another woman in the class, someone who was spiritual. But Mark persisted, badgering Marg to give me a message. It sounded exactly like the part in the movie *Ghost* when Patrick Swayze pestered Whoopi Goldberg by singing *Ninety-Nine Bottles of Beer on the Wall*, until she finally gave in to him. I knew how persistent Mark could be when he had his mind made up.

Finally, Marg agreed to help. As soon as she got home, she jotted down what Mark had instructed her to write. The note was remarkable; it started out in Marg's handwriting and then suddenly changed to what looked exactly like Mark's printing. Essentially, the note said that Mark loved us more than life itself. He wanted me to listen to *In the Arms of the Angels*, a song about a young girl who commits suicide to escape life. Instead, she finds herself safe, in the arms of the Angels. Please understand, he said, that if he was ever going to find peace, I would have to let him go.

"You were right, Mom," said Mark in the printing that was clearly his. "It was spur of the moment. No more second chances this time."

That was something that only Mark and I would understand. Marg could never have known about it.

I didn't know what to say, beyond thanking Marg for bringing me this wonderful gift. I also told her that if some stranger or anyone else had brought me this note, I might have been more skeptical. Marg was so down to earth; I believed her. As for the note, it was totally something Mark would do. Marg then handed me the Sarah McLachlan CD and said that it was part of the deal. She also confessed that she hated exercising with a passion, but was afraid that if she hadn't accepted my invitation, she would have lost her nerve and the opportunity to carry out Mark's wishes. I could just picture Mark snickering to himself while she sweated to the "Oldies" in order to accomplish her mission. He had chosen the right person.

That night I listened to the CD and gave Mark my blessing, telling him that it was time to go on.

The Little Buck Returns

A year after Mark's death, I planned a family reunion at our home. It was important for me to bring the family together, to cherish each other while we still could. Losing Mark had made me realize how fragile life is. I was sitting at our kitchen table blowing up balloons when my Mom called. I told her how much I was feeling the loss and how hard this reunion was going to be, without our Mark. No sooner had I finished my sentence than a little buck deer came strolling up the driveway.

"Oh, my God," I exclaimed. "He's come after all."

When I told Mom what had happened, she said, "Jude, I can't believe it."

A year later, Bill was demolishing our old garage. Hidden away in the rafters, he found the lost black GT racer sleigh that the boys had enjoyed while growing up. Grandma and Papa had given the boys the sleigh one Christmas. Grandma had even slid down the hill, at the back of our house, on the sleigh with the boys.

"Whatever became of the old GT snow racer?" I asked Mark one time.

"I haven't seen it for ages," he said guiltily.

It wasn't exactly a lie, but now the mystery was finally solved. The tracks were almost completely worn off because, we discovered, Mark had gotten his buddies to pull him on the sleigh behind a car. No wonder the tracks were nearly destroyed and burnt off; it was from the friction of the road. After he found the sleigh, Bill sat hunched over the picnic table, staring at it, and crying, heartbroken. That's when a visitor, in the form of the little buck, came to spend time with him.

One Thanksgiving, Bill and I built a tiny desk and stools, with a plaque dedicated to Mark. We presented it in Mark's name to the children's section of Norway Point Church in honour of his love for children. After the service, Grandma and Papa, Bill and I, were sitting at our kitchen table feeling a bit down when suddenly we saw a beautiful, full-grown buck standing in my garden, peering at us through the porch window. Mark's lonesome Papa slowly walked into the porch to get a better view, tears filling his eyes as he stared at the majestic animal that seemed to be staring back at him. I couldn't help noticing how his mourning had aged him.

"Hello, my boy," he said. "I didn't believe it, but now I feel it."

The pair spent a few precious minutes together before our special visitor wandered off. As Mark's Papa stood there, deep in thought, peering into the woods, I realized how much his personality had changed since he lost his Mark. He had lost a bit of his spark and become a little bitter. They had adored each other and had so much in common. Mark was his Papa's hope for the future. The family hunt camp also seemed to lose its luster for his Papa who had hoped Mark would carry on the family hunting tradition after Papa passed on. Now that dream was gone. Papa even seemed to resent his young nephew, Blake, who tried so desperately to please him, but couldn't replace or compensate for the loss of Mark.

Later on, Mark's Papa didn't want to join the regular gang at the family hunt camp because it was a reminder that Mark wasn't with us any longer. He set up an old trailer on his own property, took the clown caricature picture of Mark and spent the hunting season alone. The next winter, the snow load crushed the trailer, but Papa made sure he recovered the picture of Mark. This is why the caricature on page 41 looks a little the worse for wear.

On the fifth anniversary of Mark's death, when I got home from work, I asked Bill if he had seen his annual visitor. He said he had some visitors, but not the usual little buck. A doe with two beautiful little fawns had appeared instead. I suggested to Bill that this was a sign of a new beginning.

That night Tee, my daughter-in-law, phoned to announce that she was engaged. She hoped it didn't upset us because of the timing. Her husband-to-be wanted to give her a pleasant memory of August 8, to replace the horrible one that she had been carrying around all those years. I told her about the doe and fawns and assured her not to worry because she not only had our blessing, but I think she had Mark's as well.

Like the little buck, we knew Mark had finally moved on.

The Monument

For Mark's monument, we chose a picture of a couple standing by a lake, with a little buck deer watching from the distance. We also found this poem to place on the back of the stone:

The world has lost a warm and loving person
Who made a special difference every day.
Yet all those seeds of love so gently planted
Leave blossoms that will never fade away.

AUTHOR UNKNOWN

When I found this poem, I had no idea that gardening would become such an important part of my healing. I elaborated my own thoughts:

If we all take the time to plant little seeds of kindness, love, forgiveness, and patience,

I know we will reap the benefits of contentment, good friends, and feeling good about ourselves.

If we plant seeds of hate, jealousy, prejudice, anger, and blame,

We will grow a garden of bitterness, despair, hatred, loneliness, and darkness.

I hope that you all grow bountiful gardens that give you lasting joy.

Suicide

Suicide is terrible for the people left behind. Everyone feels guilty and a lot of marriages fail. Everyone wonders why they couldn't have seen it coming and why they didn't do something to prevent it. I have grown to hate that dreaded question "why"? Bill let that word consume him.

Often the test of courage is not to die but to live.

VITTORIO ALFIERI

After I lost Mark, people would often confide in me. One person told me about feeling very close to committing suicide.

"At that moment you don't think of anyone except yourself," the person said. "You don't think of how you might hurt your loved ones. You just feel in pain and want to put an end to it."

Maybe that person didn't even know why there was so much pain. Sometimes it is just a culmination of life's events that push people over the edge. If they could just ride it out, things often look better when facing a new day.

Everyone wanted an explanation.

Why did Mark take his life?

Bill wanted to blame someone, anyone but his son. It had to be somebody's fault. For me, the why wasn't as important as keeping him alive in my heart. I needed to honour his memory by telling his stories. There was no easy explanation. Some people thought that he had an undiagnosed bipolar condition. Some people thought he had an undiagnosed learning disability. Mark was very quick at picking up mechanical things, completing tasks rather than learning how to do them by following written instructions. He would often do poorly on exams, but knew the answers if asked questions orally.

When he died, all Mark's dreams were coming together, but he knew that he would have to go to night school to pick up a few more credits to take his mechanic's courses before he could apply to the fire department. Maybe he was afraid of failing.

Everyone counted on Mark and cared about him. Mark was passionate about the people he loved and he didn't want to let them down by failing. They say it's easier to have a dream than have the possibility of it actually coming true.

The night Mark left the house to meet with friends, he damaged our car. He was driving out along a cottage road and ran into a chain that a cottager had recently put across the exit. Maybe that was the straw that broke the camel's back. Maybe he felt ashamed and felt he couldn't face us. Maybe he thought he had let us down.

Knowing the reason for his actions might have helped, but it wouldn't bring him back. I think the most important thing, for those left behind, is our own survival. In death, our loved ones are at peace, but we are left to pick up the pieces. It isn't easy, but we have to move through it. Acceptance, love and forgiveness are a lot more important than knowing why. We must accept what we can't change and try to accept what happened. We must forgive ourselves and forgive the person who has taken his or her life. Only then will we be able to carry on. It isn't easy, but we have to move through it. As the saying goes: it is important to start swimming or at least tread water or we will sink.

Final Thoughts about Grieving for Mark

At one point, I felt as if I would never feel joy again. When I did begin to feel moments of happiness, I felt guilty. I wasn't supposed to laugh at a joke, or be happy, even for a moment.

I had lost my son, my Mark.

What kind of a mother was I?

When I finally got past that stage, I realized that Mark would want me to feel joy. Only then was I able to give myself permission to let some sunshine in and embrace the few moments of joy.

We all have different experiences and unique stories to tell. But there is still a common thread that bonds parents who have lost loved ones to suicide. The only people who can know how you are feeling are those who have lived it themselves. Everyone suffers differently and we all have to go through it in our own way. We can make the decision to embrace death and grief, or to honour the memory of our loved ones by embracing life.

Right now, you may be stuck in a roomful of depression and feel a sense of loss that overpowers every other sensation. Never lose hope – there is always a door in your room, or a shining light at the end of your hallway. It just takes the courage and strength to begin walking towards it. To be honest, in spite of all my support, I am no stranger to depression. Yet I consider myself one of the lucky ones; I had my work and the support of many loved ones. I had lots of opportunities to vent my grief and share my emotions. If you are not as fortunate, perhaps now is the time to join a support group. Volunteer work is another avenue to pursue. You would be surprised what you can receive while giving to others. I discovered this every day in the medical clinic.

Always keep this thought close:

> *Those we love can never really leave us. We feel their presence like a gentle touch whenever we remember moments shared and do again the things they loved to do. In so many ways, they remain with us, their gentle spirits part of all we do and all we are.*

AUTHOR UNKNOWN

THE JOURNEY
THAT FOLLOWED

Lessons of Life
While Gardening

The best place to find God is in the Garden.
You can dig for him there.

GEORGE BERNARD SHAW

Every night, Bill's mourning and drinking dragged me down. It drained every ounce of energy I had left. So every night I would seek refuge in my garden. At first, it was just an escape, but soon the garden began to give me strength. It opened my mind to new thoughts and experiences. I was surrounded by living things as I dug my way through my grief and the storms of life.

When a life-altering event occurs, we become more aware of, and appreciate, the tiny things in life. My world seemed to slow down. The magnificence of nature absorbed me, surrounding me until I was able to regain my footing. Things like the wonderful detail of a bird and its song stood out, and the song became a little sweeter. It was only natural that I would turn to gardening to help me find my way.

My garden was already a place to escape, but now it was also a place to heal and to open myself to new growth. It was a sanctuary, where I could reflect and learn acceptance, patience and understanding. Material things lost their lustre. I began to experience a deeper appreciation for the miracles of Mother Earth.

One of the first things my garden gave me was hope – hope that the flowers and plants would flourish and blossom into something beautiful. Everything seemed to die in winter. In spring, new growth appeared. This gave me hope that there was life after death. The new growth worked like a spring tonic for me. The birds were my cheering section.

My first project was the garden that Mark had started on the hill, the one that the little buck deer had inspected while Tee and I watched. I decided to make it into a memorial garden, a sign of something beautiful, to replace my disappointment and loss. It gave me a purpose. If I convinced myself that it was a gift for Mark, it gave me a reason to keep going. It didn't take long for me to learn that I handled life and gardening in the same way. I learned by trial and error.

I told my friend BF about how important gardening was becoming to me.

"Does that mean that I should be gardening?" he asked.

"Of course not," I replied. "The important thing is to enjoy nature and life in whatever form makes you happy and you will reap the benefits.

"*Life is your garden.* How you manage and tend it, is entirely up to you."

When I worked in the garden, I was surrounded by living things. I became alive and began to think about life. Suddenly my creative juices began to flow as I made plans for the placement of new plants. I was turning a bad situation into something good, by caring for living things and by making something special in Mark's memory. This gave me a purpose.

I remember reading about a study carried out in a nursing home. There were twenty elderly residents who were dying. Ten of them were given house plants to water and care for. The ten who had the plants in their rooms felt a sense of responsibility and purpose. They felt that they were making a difference and their lives were enriched by it. The residents who had plants to look after all lived longer than the other ten.

This lesson also reminds us that it is better to give, to help others, than receive. The secret is to give from your heart, without expecting anything in return. Then, and only then, will you get that special feeling of doing something good.

Another thing that gardening taught me was the importance of roots. If I planted a large plant with a good solid root system, it would usually survive because it had a healthy start and was already established. If I planted younger plants, they often perished because their roots weren't deep enough to get sufficient nourishment from the soil. This made me appreciate that I had been given a good root system, one that was established by my family history.

Mark's garden was a challenge. It was quite a distance from the house and watering it became an issue. It was also on the side of a hill that was often baked by the sun. I didn't weed it as much as I did the gardens that were closer to the house. I discovered that the young plants didn't get enough nourishment; they were like children who live in drought-stricken countries. Lacking sufficient food and water, they often withered and died.

There was one plant that I regretted putting in Mark's garden. It was tansy, a member of the yarrow family. I got the plant at a garage sale and thought it was a bargain. Not so much. The tansy was so invasive that it ended up taking over a whole section of the garden. Another friend gave me a couple of plants that had a different invasive hitchhiker attached to them. The hitchhiker also took over the garden. There was a lesson here. I learned that it sometimes pays to plan ahead, do some homework, and if you spend a little more in the beginning, you may get better results in the long run.

Weeds remind me of a children's story, told at Norway Point Church. Once there was a Grandfather who took his Grandson into his garden. He asked him to pull out three weeds, each one bigger than the one before it. The first one came out easily, the second a little harder, but the third one's roots were so deeply embedded and hard to pull out that the grandson couldn't do it.

"Why are you making me pull out these weeds?" he asked the Grandfather. "It's too difficult. What is the purpose of doing it, anyway?"

The Grandfather explained that weeds are like bad habits. At first, when they are small, they are easy to eliminate. But when weeds grow bigger, like bad habits, they become part of our personalities and are hard to break or pull out.

I also found I could pamper a plant and give it the very best of care, but sometimes it wouldn't survive. Yet a seed could fall by the wayside and it would thrive and produce a beautiful flower. I realized that we could love our children and give them the very best of care, but it didn't guarantee they would be successful or survive – for any number of reasons. The flower that surprises us, and blooms so beautifully, is the child who lives and succeeds. against all odds. Gardening is like life and sometimes it teaches us that "ours is not to reason why."

Gardening, very quickly, taught me about disappointment. I bought some expensive lily bulbs, with the hope that they would make a wonderful statement in Mark's garden. Instead, they made a hearty meal for squirrels, who dug them up when I wasn't looking. My hostas also provided a salad bar for the local deer and the slugs got the ones the deer missed. Some plants are taken over by insects or disease, just as life can be invaded by human illness.

It was ironic that later, when Jason was sick, I planted a very healthy vegetable and herb garden. I wanted to give him healthy, organic, food for fighting his cancer. The garden was just getting established and doing quite nicely, when I had a visitor one night who ate the top off every plant. There must have been a very healthy deer in the neighbourhood. Isn't it ironic that one little buck had brought us so much joy, while another brought us so much disappointment?

Once my gardens became established, I found I would often have to move plants to different locations. Some plants were hidden amongst the larger plants and were starving for sunlight or room to flourish. Once I had moved them, they shone for everyone to see. It was their turn to shine because they were given a chance. This sometimes happens to children who are being raised in the wrong environment. They often thrive when taken to a new situation.

A perfect example of this happened to one of our son's best friends. He was doing poorly in school, was the class clown and didn't do very well out of school, either. His Grandmother still lived in England. His father said if he was ever going to make anything of himself, he should move to England and live with her to make a new start. The boy agreed and the move made all the difference. His Granny was very strict and he loved and respected her; that was what he needed. He went back to school and excelled. He is now a successful chiropodist with his own practice in England. He is happily married, with a daughter who is the light of his life. This boy, also named Jason, is very special to me. He calls me all the time and I always let him know how proud I am of him.

Consistency is the most important word in gardening. Unfortunately, that isn't one of my greatest traits, so my gardens suffer. If the weeds aren't consistently kept in check, they soon take over. Small jobs then turn into a monstrous task. Deadheading, trimming and edging must be done regularly. You can always tell the difference between a garden that has a regular gardener and a garden that has a master who gets around to it every once in a while.

I thought that when I retired, I would be more consistent and have beautiful gardens. Instead, I'm travelling all over, writing this book, pondering life and enjoying my new-found freedom. My gardens are suffering terribly. They are well-established and will wait for me, like old friends, who have been ignored for a while but who know that I still care for them. We'll have some quality time one of these days. At the moment, I don't need them to survive and I guess they can survive without me for a while.

Not being consistent has affected my whole life. It ruins my attempt to diet, exercise regularly and keep up with my housework. Inconsistent people are usually never organized. I can't blame my roots, because my parents and grandparents were extremely regimented. In my defence, I now realize that I have been steadfast in things that really matter to me. I have never given up and I always keep searching for the right path.

This often requires all my energy, so other things in my life sometimes have to slide. My moral centre is held firm in the way I care for others and I understand the importance of being true to myself.

My gardens give me joy. Joy when they bloom beautifully. Joy when a favourite plant survives. Joy when I feel healthy from all the fresh air and exercise. Joy when I pull into the driveway and see the product of my hard work. Joy when I take a bouquet to someone who, in turn, can also experience the joy.

The patients in the clinic always seemed overjoyed to see the bouquets that I took into the office. They might come in feeling a bit down, but their spirits were uplifted by the hand-cut flowers at my desk. Patients often asked what kind of flowers they were, or they remarked on the vibrant colours. It seemed to take their minds off their troubles for an instant. The Norway Point Church congregation also received joy from my flower arrangements.

Jim, one of our clinic patients, could be a bit crusty at his appointments. This presented me with a bit of a challenge. Instead of giving in to his grumpiness, I joked with him. One day he showed interest in the bouquet I had on my desk and asked me what kind of flowers they were. I told him they were single peonies, which were quite rare. They had come with our old homestead.

"Those aren't peonies," Jim said. "I have pink peonies, and they don't look anything like that. I think you're full of crap!"

"Well." I replied. "I would love your kind of peonies, but I'm afraid that I'm stuck with mine."

The next time Jim came in, he walked up to my desk with a big smile on his face. He was holding one of his arms behind his back. Out came a peony plant from his garden. I gave him a big hug and said I would plant it to always remember "my big old softy, grumpy patient."

I had won him over.

Unfortunately my bouquets never brought joy to one of my co-workers. They drove her crazy because sometimes the odd bug travelled on the flowers. I also learned not to put white phlox in my bouquets because we all agreed they smelled like cat pee. I understood that it is hard to please everyone.

Gardening taught me that the best way to begin is to just get on with it. If I forced myself to go out into the garden to begin working, I soon got so involved that I wasn't tired anymore. I would soon see some progress and that made me feel good about myself.

My Dad once told me a story that he had read in *Reader's Digest*. There was a stone in the middle of a family's homestead lawn; it had been there for generations. Over the years, the family had even painted it red so they could avoid it with the lawn mower. One day, the owner's daughter got frustrated with the stone and decided to start digging it out. It turned out that the stone was just a big boulder that didn't take long to uncover and remove. She couldn't believe how much aggravation it had caused them for so many years. Someone just needed to take on the task and get started.

Much as I loved it when my gardens blossomed and flourished, what was most significant were the life lessons that gardening taught me.

When Jason got married, I was in prime gardening mode so I wrote this poem to celebrate the occasion.

Think of Your Love as a Garden:
May you water it with kindness and understanding and keep it weeded with forgiveness and patience.
May you nourish it with thoughtfulness and love and add sunshine with a sense of humour and fun.
Add good earth by expanding your minds while learning and experiencing new things. That way your soil will be healthy and your roots will grow deep.
To keep your garden blooming and beautiful, you must add new plants… in the way of new friends and possibly some little sprouts that you grow from seed.
Every garden requires hard work, but the work brings satisfaction of a job well done.

If you need a little propping up like all good flowers do,
your family will be there for support,
Take time to enjoy your garden by making time for
each other.
As you enjoy the trellis as a symbol in the garden to stay,
may you cherish your vows of love made today.

The Most Important
Garden of All

Gardening was rewarding, but I also discovered that I enjoyed just stepping outside my door and going for a walk. I could get the benefits of exercise without lifting a gardening tool. Nature, with all its miracles, is the most important garden of all. The cycle of the seasons takes care of all those tedious tasks of weeding, pruning, mulching, cultivating, replanting and landscaping. In our area, there are a variety of wonderful trails to choose from. I particularly enjoyed walks in the spring and fall.

During a Hardy Lake walk with friends in the spring, I couldn't help but marvel at the forest floor, carpeted with a new growth of dog-tooth violets, brightly-coloured moss, mayflowers and purple violets. The air was fresh and the buds on the trees were beginning to swell. It was a wonderful way to remind us that we were alive.

In autumn, I walked the Wilson Falls trail. It would be hard to beat this local trail. There is a dam at the head of the falls, with a footbridge leading over the fast-flowing water. A gentle breeze caressed my face as the musky smell of the water tickled my senses. Farther along the bank, as the river slowed to a gentle flow, I noticed the fragrances of summer's end. Bright rays of sunlight shone through the foliage, making shadows over a few scattered leaves, on the well-worn path. Halfway along the trail, I came to a stream, where I was soothed by the hypnotizing sound of water as it trickled gently over well-placed rocks which were artistically adorned with moss or ferns, before flowing into the Muskoka River. At the end of the trail, there is a flight of stairs that goes up the side of the hill which provides a healthy cardiovascular workout. It doesn't get any better than that.

Depression

When people say that depression hurts, they are absolutely right. At first, I thought I must have a serious illness; every muscle in my body ached, my head ached and I felt a tiredness that I couldn't describe. I thought that if I just had a rest, I would feel better, but it never worked. I would wake up in the morning feeling more tired than the night before. My doctor said that what I was feeling was equivalent to pneumonia. I lost my ability to concentrate and had trouble remembering words and completing sentences. I found it difficult to read books because I was unable to focus. To add to my worry, I thought that I might be developing Alzheimer's disease, which is my greatest fear.

I would drag myself out of bed in the morning, take a couple of Advil and drive to work. It helped to pop a CD in the player. Music is truly good for the soul and it always helps to increase my energy level. The minute I walked into the office, I would put a smile on my face and begin the day. The girls were always there for our morning bitch-and-laugh session. Then presto, the doctors would arrive, the patients would start coming in the door, the phones would start ringing and I didn't have time to be depressed. Without this routine, I don't know what would have happened.

I thought I was hiding my condition very nicely, but I couldn't fool my sisters. They told me that if I didn't make an appointment with my doctor, they would make one for me. With the help of antidepressants,

I managed to keep one foot ahead of the other and began to feel a little better. I made up my mind to not let depression win.

I was saddened when Robin Williams took his life. He was such an incredible talent, a man who could make people laugh. Robin was obviously a caring individual who managed, for the most part, to keep his demons of depression hidden. His personality reminded me of Mark's – they were both hardworking clowns with big hearts.

The daughter of a friend of mine was also in a very deep depression. She had trouble functioning and couldn't drag herself out of bed. A small task, like combing her hair, was too difficult. I think she was probably angry and hard on herself, which compounded her problem. Her therapist said that she should celebrate the little things she could accomplish instead of beating herself up for what she didn't accomplish. She needed to start with baby steps. With the help of medication and therapy, she slowly began to recover. Hearing this story made me grateful that my own depression was so minor compared to hers. There are always people worse off than we are. I saw it every day at the doctor's office and that helped me cope and be thankful for the blessings I had. We must never take them for granted.

Another friend told me about one of her friends, who had lost her son in a tragic skiing accident. His body was lost in an avalanche. Every weekend, his parents went to the site to search. It was months before his body was discovered. The mother could not deal with the pain of losing her son and spent five years consumed with mourning and depression. Leaving her home became difficult. Finally, realizing she needed help, she made an appointment to see a therapist. The therapist's home was in a picturesque setting surrounded by gardens. As the woman walked down the path towards the house, she was stopped in her tracks by the sight of a beautiful magnolia tree in full bloom. She couldn't help staring at it; the tree was so magnificently gorgeous. When the therapist introduced herself, the mother told her how she had been entranced by her beautiful tree.

"If you can take two minutes to find some joy in the wonder of nature, those are the first two minutes towards your recovery," the therapist said.

By itself, medication isn't the answer. It's just a helping hand to begin recovery. A drawback that I experienced was the feeling of being emotionally flat and being unable to weep. Since I have ceased the antidepressants, I still have trouble finishing sentences, but I celebrate every time my eyes fill with tears.

My support group of sisters, friends and co-workers also helped me build confidence in myself. Dr. Kent was a great supporter. He encouraged me to start walking, and to join the gym. I also had a great deal of respect for him and didn't want to let him down. He gave me good advice; when I went for a walk and exercised, I felt better. He also kept reminding me that fruit and vegetables were my friends. He was right again. We all know a healthy diet makes us feel better. We also know that life often gets in the way. Maintaining a healthy lifestyle is a constant uphill battle. I'm still trudging along.

Many of us put ourselves down and need others to prop us up and give us confidence. Everyone has some talent to bring to the table. I hope that you will be as lucky as I have been, to have people who will remind you of your redeeming qualities. Always think of your assets instead of your faults. When you recognize your assets, you can build on them.

I now feel that I was meant to write this book. When I told Sal that I was about to get it published, she said, "Oh, Jude, the next thing we know you'll be opening an antique shop!"

Don't you love it? That's my pal.

All we have is this moment. Yesterday is history. There is nothing we can do about the past, except learn from it. We cannot fully enjoy the present until we let go of the bad moments in our lives and we release them. We often spend senseless energy brooding about the future, about things that might happen, but usually never do.

When my Mom was diagnosed with lymphoma, the family was understandably very upset. Jason, in particular, had trouble accepting it. When he lost his brother, he became very frightened of death. Who would have guessed that both Jason and my Dad would die before Mom? So again, the important lesson is to seize the moment because that is all any of us have. Life can change in a heartbeat. We are all going to die. The important part is how we live our "dash" – the mark on our tombstone between our birth date and our date of death. I hope I still have enough "dash" left to at least hold this finished book in my hands.

Sally once told me that when her Mom died she thought the world would stop turning, but it didn't. Then, she realized that as long as the world does keep turning on its axis, we must keep moving with it. She was right.

Meditation Course

My friend BF and another friend took a meditation course and recommended that I take it as well. They thought it would help me move into a better place. We are fortunate to have Dr. Bill Knight in our area, a physician who has proven that meditation helps cut medical costs, so the course could be covered by the Ontario Health Insurance Plan. The course involves a commitment to eight weekly sessions, two interviews, and one full-day session. Like anything else in life, the more you put into meditation, the more you will get out of it. Meditation teaches us to control our breathing and to be more aware and mindful of the moment. The program helps people to completely relax, improve their concentration, relieve stress, and help manage pain.

Everyone who takes the course must have an interview with Dr. Knight before and after the program. In my interview before the course, he asked me to describe how I was feeling at that very moment. I told him that I saw myself, as a colourful and smiling, hollow clown marionette made of wood. I was dancing, but I was controlled by strings. I had a large smile painted on my wooden face, but inside there was only a skeleton surrounded by a dead, empty, shell. For a moment, I wondered where that image came from. It was then I realized that the image represented exactly how I was feeling at the time. It was me, putting on a good front for everyone; but I had lost my essence and vitality and was only a shell of my former self. The strings represented the fact that I was always trying to stay in control, please everyone else and was tied to my responsibilities. In the middle of the course, I noticed that my face always hurt when I was meditating.

When I mentioned it to Dr. Knight, he suggested that my face hurt because I was always wearing a mask.

Interesting.

The course must have made a difference. Dr. Knight asked me how I was feeling in my last interview.

"I feel like I am walking in a forest surrounded by friends," I said.

Sometime after the course, Dr. Knight visited my gardens, as part of a local garden tour. When I confessed that I hadn't been keeping up my meditation, as much as I had planned, he said not to worry. My gardens were giving me inner peace and time to be mindful of the moment. He was right.

Meditation has been a wonderful tool for my healing journey. The world is moving so quickly these days. In the midst of our busy lives, with our heads full of thoughts, it is important to take time to slow down, to concentrate on the moment and step into a quiet place inside to regroup. Meditation helps me focus. I am afraid that I don't have a regular meditation routine, but I try to practice my breathing several times a day. Take a large breath in through your nose for a count of four, hold it for a count of four, then slowly release the breath by blowing it out slowly through your mouth. If you repeat the process several times, it will help stop your mind from racing, release some tension and give you a little shot of energy. The odd time, when I'm eating alone, I make a point of savouring each bite, chewing very slowly to appreciate the flavours, textures and consistency of the food. It is another way to enjoy the moment. We often devour our food without even realizing how much, or what, we have eaten. Now that I am in a better place in my life, I would like to retake the course. I think I would get even more out of it.

The Adventures of Running a Bed and Breakfast

Five years after we lost Mark, things began spiraling downwards. I could no longer deal with Bill's negativity and drinking. None of my survival strategies were working. I knew it was time to open a new doorway, to make a new beginning. The tension at home and my unhappiness were beginning to affect my health. If anything, losing Mark made me realize that life is too short to waste.

Everything came to a head one Friday night when I gave Bill the news that I needed out of our marriage. He refused to accept it. Of course, he didn't see what my problem was. After all, he said, I was lucky because he always had supper ready when I came home at night. What more could I possibly want? And he didn't think he had a drinking problem since he ran his own contracting business. He just didn't get it. That was always our problem: he never got me, and I guess I never got him.

I tried to stay strong and not back down. Bill said that he would do anything to make me stay. He would even quit drinking for a year if that would make a difference. I told him that I didn't know if it would; I would always be afraid that he would start again. I had lost so much respect for him, especially since we lost Mark and I didn't know if I would ever get it back. Finally, I gave in. I would give him one last chance. We had gone through this so many times before; I always took him back.

It was a difficult weekend. Bill kept his promise, but by Sunday night, he had a hard battle with withdrawal. Our new life of sobriety had begun. After a few weeks, Bill began to change. He started showing interest in life again. Previously, by the time supper was over, Bill was dozing in a chair, but now we could actually have a conversation. I told him that if we were going to build a new life together, we had to begin making some changes. We had to leave the past behind and start building a future. We needed something positive to work on.

We had always talked about starting a bed and breakfast after the kids had grown, as a part of a retirement plan. Now, it seemed, was the time to do it. I decided to make an investment in our future and cashed all my RRSPs to renovate the house to make it more appealing as a bed and breakfast. If our marriage didn't work out, I thought, I couldn't go wrong by improving the house for future resale. Besides, designing and working on renovation projects has always given me pleasure and a sense of accomplishment.

I told Bill that our first project would be renovating Mark's bedroom. He would be happy that we were doing something positive together. I suggested that we make it smaller, and add a bathroom for the B & B guests. Bill thought that was impossible, but our nephew, who is a plumber and electrician, agreed that nothing was impossible. We worked out a plan together. I loved working beside Bill on something positive, to see him feel good about himself. The room turned out fine, and we were now ready to start another project.

We replaced the old rickety staircase with a nice solid, straight one. The old staircase was handy when the boys were teenagers because I could always hear the steps creaking when they were trying to sneak in after a late night. The other staircase had a two-inch slant to one side because our old pioneer homestead foundation had settled over the years.

The dining room came next. We gutted the whole room and covered the brick fireplace with a white wood design. We kept the shape of the two old, curved windows but replaced them with new, efficient ones that also eliminated the old storm windows that we had to take on and off each change of season. There were also two outside doors, leading from the dining room onto the veranda, which we replaced with full glass doors. The new doors not only let in more light, but stopped the winter drafts.

Finally, we replaced the old floor with new birch hardwood. We painted the walls oat yellow with white trim. It was a good-sized room and there was enough space to put a loveseat and chairs facing the fireplace. The guests could sit there in the morning, before or after they finished breakfast. Bright and cheery with a cozy cottage look, it turned out to be one of my favourite rooms in the house. Our guests could see the lake as they enjoyed their breakfast.

We replaced the floor in our bedroom, as well as the screened-in porch off our bedroom. Then we gave the adjoining bathroom a face-lift. This would be "The Sunset Room," the most expensive since it was about fourteen by twenty-two feet with a private bathroom, fireplace and private screened-in porch that faced the lake. We moved into the tiniest bedroom down the hall – it was for a good cause!

The old place was taking shape. We had accomplished more in Bill's year of sobriety than we had in the last fifteen years. We were ready to start the B & B, but we weren't retired just yet. Since everyone told us that it can take years to build up that kind of business, we thought we would give it a try. We didn't even know if running a B & B was for us.

We got our first chance to practice one weekend when the lodge next door to us had an overflow. Jason was home for a visit, so we warned him we were having our first customers. He was not impressed.

"I don't know how you can let strangers stay in your house," he told us while we were standing in the driveway saying goodbye. "Are you sure you want to do this?"

I told him not to worry because B & B guests were a special kind of people. Everything would be just fine. Just then we heard the roar of two Harley Davidson motorcycles pulling in our driveway. Jay gave me a look. I just grinned and shrugged my shoulders.

The three riders were dressed in their black leathers and I had no idea what to expect. They turned out to be a husband and wife, who arrived with a friend. The man was a lawyer and they were visiting their son, who was staying at the lodge for the summer, while he worked at Bigwin Inn. They were great people, and we enjoyed our first B & B experience very much. I phoned Jay on Sunday night to let him know that we were safe, and that I was right – our guests were wonderful.

I designed some brochures, did some research, and began working on a plan to start our new adventure. Both the Muskoka and Canadian B & B associations had good websites, so we decided that we would list with them the next spring. The doctors agreed to give me July and August off to see how it went. We knew that summer in the Muskoka area would be the busiest time of year. The rest of the time, we could just stay open on weekends.

We planned a sisters' weekend to celebrate. The morning before I left on my holiday, we ran out of water while I was having my shower. The pump, in the bottom of our three-hundred-foot, drilled well had burned out. I had to leave Bill with the problem. He got a couple of our neighbours to give him a hand to get the pump out of the well in order to replace it. Our nephew, the plumber, came to install the new pump and helped to finish the job. When they finally got the water flowing once again, Bill decided to have a beer to celebrate and to relax the tension. Our neighbour Ted begged him not to do it, but Bill assured him that he would only have one and he wouldn't let it get out of control. I was devastated when I arrived home Sunday afternoon to find that the boom had fallen once again. My first thought was to blame myself – if I hadn't gone away for the weekend, things might have been different. Then I realized that Bill was a grown man who didn't need a babysitter. If it hadn't happened that weekend, it likely would happen another time.

Despite this setback, we were committed to the project. The summer arrived and the minute we opened the doors, we were booked every night. It was amazing. I had always loved the lake and sitting on the dock, but Bill hated the water and didn't understand what it meant to me. As the guests started coming, however, I think we both learned to appreciate what we had. We took guests down to the dock and they would all say how lucky we were to have this piece of heaven. Bill began to realize it too, and started to enjoy sitting on the dock. He also fit into the role of a B & B host quite well. He enjoyed cooking and was the organized one of the family, so we made a good team.

Another big difference between the two of us is that I love to travel, but Bill enjoys being at home. At the time we opened the B & B, we couldn't afford to travel, so I enjoyed the guests from faraway places the most. I thought, well, if I couldn't go to visit them, at least they could come to me. Listening to their stories and hearing about their customs was so interesting; it was like taking trips to different parts of the world. After breakfast, I would ask guests to mark their hometowns, with an X, in my Atlas.

The fact that we were within thirty minutes of the magnificent Algonquin Provincial Park – one of Canada's National Historic Sites – was a draw for a lot of European travelers. I remember one couple from The Netherlands who drove to Algonquin Park every day in hopes of seeing a moose. The man ended up thinking that the moose-crossing signs were some sort of propaganda because he didn't believe that moose existed in Canada. One morning, after he had left for Algonquin, I saw three moose standing on the road on my drive to work. He found it hard to believe me. I explained that it was just a matter of being at the right place, at the right time. He finally bought a small stuffed moose for a souvenir. He didn't speak English very well and got a kick out of how I talked. I booked him a one-day canoe trip in Algonquin Park. When I hung up the phone, I said, "Here's the scoop." He had no idea what I meant, so I explained that I was telling him what the plan was for his outing. After they finished their coffee, on the veranda, they wanted me to take their picture.

"Snuggle up so I can get a good picture," I said.

"What do you mean snuggle?" the man asked.

It was fun. A week later, we got an email from them when they were back in The Netherlands. They thanked us for a great holiday and said, "Here's the scoop."

They wrote that they had been upgraded to first class on the way home and were now snuggling up on the couch, looking at the pictures from their wonderful vacation.

I was surprised that we had so many guests from Israel. A lot of them were Russian Jews who had escaped to Israel. It also amazed me how many languages most Europeans speak. It made me feel a little inadequate. I asked a couple of visitors from Israel how they ended up coming all this way and how they found us. They explained that in Israel they were surrounded by their enemies, so the only way they could have a relaxing holiday was to get on a plane and fly somewhere far away. Our location appealed to them because we were situated between Ottawa, Algonquin Park, and Toronto. They thought that we were very lucky to live in Canada. When they showed us a picture of their grandchildren, playing in a lovely playground, they told us that there were soldiers armed with machine guns just out of sight of the camera. The man said people never totally felt safe in Israel. I was amazed. It was certainly a wakeup call; we should appreciate our home even more.

One of our special guests worked for Iran Air. Her parents, who were visiting her in Toronto from Iran, had never been out into the country, so she booked them a weekend in the Sunset Room. The parents couldn't speak a word of English and seemed very shy. When Bill and I walked down to the dock in the afternoon, they were sitting there, in long-sleeved clothing, having a picnic. Through her daughter, the mother asked us whether we felt safe here, which really took me aback. Of course, I felt safe here, I answered, *very* safe. The old man smiled, pointing to the lake and made a diving motion. Since I was in my bathing suit, I humoured him, and took a running dive off the end of the dock. He got a kick out of it. I thought, afterwards, that what seemed so acceptable and normal, for a woman to do here, would have probably meant severe punishment for her in Iran.

That same night, we welcomed two visitors from Scotland and a professor from England with his daughter and her husband, from New York. This wasn't long after 9/11 (September 11, 2001). At breakfast, the next morning, as I prepared for everyone to sit around the round dining room table, I told them that we also had visitors from Iran. When the Iranian guests came down, they were hesitant about sitting with everyone else. I assured them that they were welcome. I said it was like a mini–United Nations and that I should have flags in front of each place. There were pleasant conversations about the weather in each country, as well as about the various customs and holidays. At the end of breakfast, I made a toast to my guests and said that, if there were more B & Bs, there would be less fighting and unrest in the world. Before the Iranians left, the daughter insisted that I come up to inspect their room. I didn't understand why at first, but soon realized that she was being cautious. She didn't want to be accused of stealing, or vandalism. Again, I realized how much we take our freedom for granted. The whole weekend was very eye-opening for me. As they were pulling out of the yard, I waved goodbye. The old man rolled down his window and with a big smile, made a diving motion with his hands. What a great experience.

I also remember a very uptight lady from California, who came with her friend. They had come all that way to go to Bigwin Island for supper because she had been a nanny to a family in the area when she was a teenager. She was now married to a restaurant critic in California. She and her friend were exhausted from their road trip and were in quite a state. She seemed to complain about everything. When I showed them to their room, I asked them if a gin and tonic would help them relax. They accepted, so I fixed them a drink. I took some other guests down to the dock, and on the way back from the lake, I saw my uptight guests sitting in the screened in porch off their bedroom. I waved. They waved their glasses back and seemed to be having a great time. The Lake of Bays and the gin were working their magic already.

The next day I took them for a drive to find the cottage where she had worked. I was familiar with the family who lived there because Bill used to plow their driveway. I had their phone number in London and called them to let them know their former nanny was staying at our B & B. They really enjoyed talking to each other.

The supper at Bigwin went over well. All and all, despite the challenge, I felt great that I had won them over. I even got a nice letter from California, with some pictures of Bigwin Island taken in the 1950s, when she had worked in the area. I learned that you should never jump to conclusions about someone.

Another wakeup call came from a new set of Russian Jewish visitors. One couple didn't speak English very well and when I asked them if they would like to sit on the loveseat in the dining room, they seemed hesitant and uncomfortable. I asked them if there was a problem and the woman explained that, in Russia, they would never put a couch with the back to an open door. Where they came from, they said, they always placed a couch facing the doorway. That way, if someone came in with a firearm, they could hit the floor quickly. Yet another reminder of how we take our life and freedom for granted.

Some of my favourite guests were the climate-change scientists from Italy, who stopped for a few days, on their way to Vancouver for a Global Warming Conference. Bill was away that weekend and I was just beginning to think that they weren't going to show up. They called from Algonquin Park to get driving instructions and didn't arrive until nearly 11 p.m. The scientists could speak English, but their spouses couldn't. As soon as they arrived, Luigi rubbed his belly and they asked where they could find a restaurant to have dinner. I told them they were out of luck – nothing would be open at that hour – but I could make them something in a pinch. I opened a bottle of wine to welcome them, and whipped up some toasted western sandwiches with cheese and veggies on the side and lots of coffee cake for dessert. I asked them how they chose us. The woman replied that when she saw the word *cozy* on the website she decided ours was the place for them. She said that we were right, it was cozy. After breakfast we went for a walk in the forest behind the house. They enjoyed looking at the different flora. After our walk, they said they were going to explore for the day, but that night, they wanted to come back and cook me dinner since I had cooked for them the night before. They said that they would particularly enjoy cooking on a Canadian barbeque. That evening, they came in laden with groceries.

"Sit. Tonight you are our guest in your home," one of our guests insisted.

It was wonderful watching them working so well together. They made the dinner into an adventure. They served small courses and wine, and the conversation continued into the evening. I felt as if I had had a little taste of Italy, in my own home.

In the fall, we had another couple from The Netherlands. When they walked down to the lake to see the coloured leaves, the man saw our canoe.

"You have a Canadian boat. Can I take it out?" he asked.

I told him sorry, because the water was getting very cold and he was too inexperienced. The next day they walked back down to the lake and the man came back, wet and frozen. He said that he hadn't been able to resist trying our Canadian boat. It had tipped but he didn't care, because his wife had taken a good video to take back home. I got him a towel and he boldly stripped outside and came in wearing only the towel. We chalked that up to one more experience as B & B hosts.

A week later, I went to Toronto to help my girlfriend with her daughter's wedding. The wedding guests had rooms in a hotel near the Distillery District. The morning after the wedding, I was taking the elevator to meet the rest of the wedding guests in the restaurant downstairs, when who should I see standing in the elevator but my two Dutch guests. The man was carrying a two-foot canoe.

"Judy," he exclaimed, "What are you doing here? We are just on our way back to the airport. You said that this is a big country but it can't be because here you are. Look, I bought a Canadian boat!"

When the elevator door opened downstairs, my girlfriend couldn't figure out why I was laughing, and why I was so friendly with the people in the elevator. I introduced her to my B & B guests. My girlfriend said that she couldn't take me anywhere without me running into someone I knew.

We took pictures with my former guests, as a keepsake. When I got home on Sunday night, and checked my email, there was the picture from our special send-off. What are the chances?

A friend of ours gave her parents a weekend at the B & B as an anniversary gift. We wanted to give them a celebration, so we invited them to a barbeque on the dock with other friends. When the party was over, we all walked up from the dock at dusk and went to bed an hour later. Lying in bed, I could hear furniture moving around, and wondered why our guests would be moving things at that time of night. The next morning, when we got up, we noticed the fridge was knocked over in the sunroom. A chair had tumbled over and there were peaches strewn all over the floor. The window screen had been ripped open.

It wasn't our guests after all. It was a bear!

We had forgotten to close the windows and I'd left a basket of peaches on the top of the fridge. It was just too tempting. The bear had tipped the fridge over on its door, and couldn't figure out how to get it open – that was fortunate because there were four dozen eggs in the fridge that hadn't broken. He ate some peaches, knocked a few other things over, then went out the same window he came in. Although the fridge was ruined, he could have done a lot more damage. The paw marks he left on the pine window sill made a great story for our guests. Our friends bought us a gift of a B&B business card holder adorned with a bear ornament. It was a fun memory.

I really got a kick out of our four guests from Austria. The older woman was very paranoid and never let her purse out of her sight. She came down to breakfast every morning with it tucked tightly under her arm. One morning, our guests asked about bears, so I told them the story of the bear that got into our back porch and showed them the scratch marks on the window sill. The other three guests had to translate the story for the older woman, who didn't speak any English.

Later that night, I had trouble sleeping because her husband was snoring so loudly. All at once I heard a crash, and opened our bedroom door, to see a man's bare behind disappearing through the bathroom door. The guest had fallen, but yelled that he was fine and came out wearing just a towel. The next day, at breakfast, they were all speaking German and laughing loudly. The man who had fallen told me that he was sneaking to the bathroom, without any clothes on, when he turned the wrong way, and slipped. When he heard me open my door, he flew into the bathroom. Meanwhile, the paranoid woman was awakened by all the noise and thought there was a bear in the house. She said she was scared to death. No wonder they were all laughing.

One time, we got a call from a restaurant in Dorset, a little tourist village about ten miles away. They had a couple of stranded travelers there, and wondered if I could pick them up to spend the night. Apparently, I had to bring the truck because they had a couple of bikes with them. I was curious as I made the ten-minute trip to Dorset. The two people waiting for me were exhausted and totally covered in mud. Their only belongings were their two bicycles. Apparently, the woman and her boyfriend had taken their four-wheel-drive truck onto a back road and didn't realize that it turned into a snowmobile trail. They were in the middle of nowhere when their truck got bogged down, in a muddy swamp and their only alternative was to take the bikes they had in the back of the truck and start walking and biking, to look for help. It was dark by the time they found their way to Dorset.

I took them to our place, found the young woman some clean clothes and a nightgown and gave her boyfriend one of Bill's jogging suits and another set of clean clothes for the next day. They couldn't wait to have a shower and I gave them two new toothbrushes. The young woman, who was a nurse, said that she couldn't believe a little thing like a toothbrush could make her so happy. The next morning the young man came down in Bill's clothes. The pants were about eight inches too short and looked like clam diggers. Bill had some idea where the truck might be, made some calls to a couple of local guys who owned four-wheelers and winches and they all headed back to the site. Men love a challenge like that. Meanwhile, the young nurse and I connected and had a wonderful visit. The truck arrived back home around lunchtime, completely covered in mud, but otherwise in good running order. I had their clothes washed for the trip home. We had made two more friends and had another good B & B story.

B & B guests are an unusual breed. They are all adventurers who enjoy meeting new people, don't mind sharing a bathroom, or doing without a television. During the seven years that we ran the B & B, I only met one guest who was a bit of a problem.

One day we got a call from some cottagers, who booked a room for their parents. They came with the older couple to check out the room and get the parents settled before they took them back to the cottage for the evening. They seemed nice. I waited up for them because they needed help up the stairs when they got back. When they finally returned to the house, it was late, but I made them comfortable and got them both safely up to the room. It was after 11 p.m. when I finally got to bed myself, only to hear the phone ring. It was the children, making sure that Mom and Dad had made it back safely. I told them that they were all tucked in for the night. Things were finally settling down again when I heard a noise coming from the kitchen downstairs. I snuck down the stairs in my nightgown to see what was going on. What I found was the old gentleman – I'm using the term "gentleman" loosely – looking in the fridge. I asked if I could help him, and he said that his wife wanted a drink of juice, so I told him that I would be glad to get it for her.

Without warning, he came over to me and said, "I love you. I can't keep my hands off you."

Yikes. I didn't know what to say. Then he actually started chasing me around the kitchen and asked me to sit in the dining room with him. I told him, "No way!" in no uncertain terms and said that it was time for him to get to bed. It was quite a challenge to hold the glass of juice, hold onto my nightgown and get the man and myself up the stairs safely. In the end, his wife didn't want the juice, anyway. My stars!

I finally got into bed, one more time, while Bill snored quietly in a peaceful sleep. The next morning, when the couple came down for breakfast, the old poop was nice as pie and acted as if nothing had happened. When the children came to pick them up, he insisted on having them take a picture of me with him. He handed me a business card, telling me to get in touch if I was ever in the city for lunch. Like that was ever going to happen! There's no fool like an old fool.

Most B & B hosts don't like having bridal parties as guests because it's usually a lot of trouble. I was the opposite – I loved having wedding parties. Maybe it's the mother in me, or my romantic inner self, but I was thrilled with all the excitement and the planning. We had the bride, the bridesmaids, and the mother of the bride getting ready at our place on two separate occasions. One party had a hairdresser and a manicurist set up in the screened porch. The father of the bride showed up with the photographer for pictures. The house bustled with activity. I supplied aspirins and an ironing board, pinned on corsages, zipped up dresses and sewed a hem or a button when necessary. Another time, I even got to stand in for the father of the bride and walked her down the aisle on the night of the rehearsal.

One good thing about weddings is that everyone leaves for the wedding and they don't return until very late at night. I always enjoyed the stories about the wedding at breakfast the next morning.

We only had one bride and groom who booked for their wedding night. The young groom wanted everything to be perfect and dropped off a bottle of champagne and a dozen roses. He asked me to make a path of rose petals leading to the bedroom and sprinkle some on the bed. He said he would phone me when they arrived at the dock from Bigwin Island so I could drive down to pick them up. I felt like a wedding cupid. When he made the call, I was to make sure that the champagne was chilled, the candles were lit, the rose petals were spread and the rest of the roses were placed in a vase in the room. I also added some strawberries and whipped cream, as a final touch. The bride was very pleased with her new husband's thoughtfulness.

We also had a very romantic couple who weren't married. They also brought strawberries, whipped cream and champagne. That night, we had overbooked by mistake, and Bill and I ended up sleeping in the family room below them. There wasn't a lot of insulation in the floor and we could hear a lot of movement in the bedroom above. At first, we got a kick out of it, but by about three in the morning, I had the pillow over my head and was screaming to myself, "Enough already". Then they went into the jacuzzi tub.

The next morning, I can tell you, they had a very tired hostess serving breakfast. For their part, they looked quite refreshed. Go figure. I didn't let on that I had heard them. When they left, I was changing the four-poster bed in their room, when I found that the fancy foot bar between the two posts had been broken. It was another good story. The next week, I got several calls from the girl's girlfriends wondering if we had any rooms available. They said their girlfriend reported that ours was a very romantic B & B.

Another wedding party made a big difference in our lives. Heather and Peter were cottage neighbours who stayed on Lake of Bays for the summer, wintered in Cyprus and spent the rest of their time in the UK. Their son was coming from England, with his fiancé, to get married on Bigwin Island. Heather and Peter had rented the B & B for their cousins, who were attending the wedding. As usual, it was fun watching everyone get ready for the wedding and the next day, listening to all the great stories.

I felt an immediate closeness to one couple, Joyce and David. They stayed a couple of days longer after the wedding, so we invited Heather and Peter over for a drink to celebrate the weddings success with their cousins. After that weekend, we always made a point of getting together whenever they were in the area. On one long weekend, Joyce and

David and their friends took over the entire B & B. It gave Bill and me an opportunity to take my Mom and Dad away on a holiday. It worked out perfect. Our holiday was paid for and they looked after the B&B.

The couples had planned a pirate-themed weekend. Joyce told us that they must have looked strange, heading down to the dock, all decked out in pirate costumes. Peter and Heather picked up the hardy crew in their pontoon boat, complete with a Jolly Roger flag.

"Yo-ho-ho and a bottle of rum!" as they say.

The night we arrived home, Joyce seemed to linger until everyone went to bed so she could have a quiet chat with me. She confessed that she had cancer. I felt terrible – she was so full of energy and fun. She didn't want to waste a minute, which is the same way Jason dealt with his cancer diagnosis. Her husband bought her a red, hard-topped, convertible and they started taking trips all around the world. Later, when Jason died, she came for a visit and gave me a round candle holder with stars and moons on it. I pointed out that it was a perfect gift – Jay loved stars and moons and had a moon tattooed on one hand and a star on the other. They had a special meaning for him. Around the candle holder were the words, "Look deep within for stars lie hidden in your soul". Joyce lost her battle with cancer a couple of months later. I still have her little candle holder sitting on my dresser, as a reminder of our friendship, and her gallant fight.

We made a lot of friends while running the B & B. Roz and Lynne and their daughter Beth came to stay often. They loved the area so much that they bought a lot on a tiny lake in the area and built a cottage there. They came up on a lot of weekends so we could spend time looking at the plans and listening to all their ideas. We were their first guests invited to see their new lot and to eat hot dogs cooked over an open fire. It was fun watching their cottage go from a concept to their finished dream. They have now become family and never miss a visit when they are at their cottage.

Jim and Agnes were another couple we became close to. They built a cottage on Bigwin Island and they stayed at the B & B while the cottage was being built. Jim bought a boat and left it at our dock. Agnes and I got to go for the maiden voyage with him. They attended one of Jason's fundraisers. We have a lot of good memories from their visits.

Cathy and Peter were another set of regulars who became friends. They once showed up a week early and we told them we were totally booked. They were happy to sleep on the cot and the chesterfield in the family room. They also fell in love with Lake of Bays and now have their own cottage on the lake. We still stay in touch.

Just before Jay got sick, the B & B was getting too much for me to handle. I didn't feel right taking the summers off work and I couldn't handle both working at the clinic, and taking care of the B & B. I was beginning to feel a bit burnt out; I couldn't do a good job juggling both.

Besides, I never slept very well when we had guests – I always had to make sure that they were in bed safe and sound. It's a mom thing. Bill could go to sleep under almost any conditions.

After Jay got sick, the issue was decided for me: the B & B had to go. Bill was upset because he was really enjoying it. He loved having people around and he enjoyed cooking his old-fashioned Bill breakfasts. But when it became more of a burden than a pleasure, I knew it had to end.

Bill didn't do the laundry or change the beds, or scrub the bathrooms. He very seldom vacuumed, either. He thought I spent too much time and money on the gourmet-style breakfasts that I enjoyed making and presenting on antique dishes. We had a small difference of opinion. I enjoyed going that little extra mile for the guests. If I couldn't do it right, I didn't want to do it at all.

Bill was also drinking quite heavily again and I was on edge.

We had made wonderful memories, and followed our dream of running a successful B & B. My view was that it was fun while it lasted and we had learned a lot from our guests. Bill became less prejudiced because he realized that people from all over the world could be special, caring souls. He even accepted same-sex marriages because he got to know the people as individuals. After all, prejudice is often just fear of the unknown. Running the B & B gave us some time to sooth our souls and a respite to prepare for the next leg of our journey. Bill and I shared many special memories, working together, with a common interest.

It helped rekindle our marriage. I have no regrets. We took down the "Lake of Bays B & B" sign and began the next chapter of our lives.

****

The picture we used for the B & B logo (see page 83) was drawn by Karen Little, a cottage neighbour. Karen was a cancer survivor, but one of the things that cancer took away from her was her desire to paint. One day, when Karen was walking past our house, she was overcome with a desire to sketch the old homestead. She completed this wonderful drawing. Creating it awakened her artistic passion, once again. Unfortunately, she later lost her second battle with cancer. I am thankful that this picture will keep her memory alive for us. The picture was purchased for us as a surprise, to celebrate an occasion, by another neighbour Brenda Paterson. Thank you, Brenda.

JASON

Jason's Life

Our older son, Jason, preferred to let Mark take centre stage, but he was very special in his own way. When he was born, he was our pride and joy, and the first grandson for my parents.

He was a serious baby. When people tried to make him smile, he would just stare at them. What we didn't realize is that he was having trouble focusing; he needed glasses by the time he was two.

Almost from the beginning, Jason fought sleep. I would try rocking him, rubbing his back, giving him a bottle, but nothing worked. My girl-friend Sandy's little girl was a perfect little sleeper and Sandy insisted that I was going about it the wrong way. She told me to just let him cry for a while, to break the habit. When Jason was about eleven months and just crawling, Sandy and her husband came over to give us support to try it her way. I tucked Jason in and gently closed the door between the hallway and the living room. I sat on pins and needles while we waited in the living room. The crying began, then stopped, then began again, and stopped. It seemed to be getting louder each time. Suddenly, we heard a tapping at the living room door. Jason had somehow gotten himself over the rail of his crib and crawled down the hallway to the living room. To this day, we have no idea how he did it without hurting himself. Sandy just threw her hands up in the air in disbelief. Jason had won his first battle. I told Jay this story when he was ill. He just smiled with satisfaction and said, "Right on."

Along with his evident strong will, Jay also had a vivid imagination and artistic personality. His love of hats lasted his whole life. On his third birthday, every guest brought him a different kind of hat. He had always dreamed of being a super hero; we went through the Batman, Sherlock Holmes, GI Joe and Mr. T stages. When company came to the house and said hello to him, he would answer by saying something like, "I'm not Jason. I'm Spiderman."

When Jay was about twelve, he began the rock star stage, something he never grew out of. His first rock band consisted of four neighbourhood kids, with cardboard and wooden guitars, lip-syncing to Michael Jackson. Jason and his friend Jamie loved playing guitar so much that Jamie's dad, Jim, gave them lessons. The boys never looked back. Jason saw Jim years later and never missed a chance to thank him for starting it all.

As children, Jay hated it when Mark copied him. It was important for him to be his own person. He loved the word *unique*. In about Grade 5, he had a black tooth, longish hair and glasses that were always lopsided. He wore chains, vests and leather bracelets. One day, I tried to discourage him from dressing this way by telling him that it made him look kind of scary and not very friendly.

"Great," he said. "Then nobody will pick on me."

I guess he was using the Fonz approach.

By the time Jay got into high school, his tooth was fixed and he didn't need glasses. He became quite a handsome ladies' man. He loved playing in several rock bands and got his first job in a restaurant. He was also taking classes in culinary arts and his passion for cooking began to evolve. Jason was coming into his own.

He had a habit of bringing home stray kids for a weekend. A couple of these kids ended up staying for six months. Usually, we made a deal that they could stay as long as they kept up with their school work. Two of his friends managed to get their Grade 12 diploma before they left. Jason even brought home two budgies that needed a place to stay. Guess who ended up looking after them?

After high school, Jay worked at a local factory by day, and played his guitar and cooked by night. Over the years, Jay had a lot of girlfriends and they all remained his friends. Once we attended a wedding and I teased him about the fact that he had dated all the bridesmaids.

At the same time that he was coming into his own, Jason spent his life battling his fears. He hated to perform and was sick before a lot of public school concerts. One year, during a performance on stage, he made sure that he was standing behind the Christmas tree. From time to time, he would poke his head out and wave to me.

To his teacher's surprise, he did end up becoming a performer. He said that he learned to hide behind his guitar and was just mastering singing on stage before he got ill. His strategy for singing was to become a part of his guitar.

Jason worked hard to face his fears, one by one. He was afraid of amusement park rides so he kept going to Canada's Wonderland until he conquered them all. He was afraid of heights, so he worked at climbing the Dorset Lookout Tower until he finally made it to the top several times. He was afraid of flying, but he still took trips on planes. He told me that he was afraid because he felt out of control, but if he was flying the plane, there wouldn't be a problem.

My boys had a strange relationship. Apparently, when Jay attended Mark's stag party, he had too much to drink, partly because he felt out of place with Mark's friends. Mark lived within walking distance of the party hall and helped Jason back to his house. It was probably a bit like the blind leading the blind. It must have been quite a comedy act – at one point, Mark piggy-backed Jay. Mark was upset with him, but still loved him and looked out for him. They were brothers.

Jason's pride and joy was his long hair. He said he was going to have long hair until he was at least seventy. On Mark's wedding day, Jay showed up with a very short neat haircut. It was his ultimate sacrifice for his brother.

Grandma and Papa never missed a Christmas from the time the boys were born. They shared a special bond with them during the holiday season. Christmas lost its magic after we lost Mark. We all tried to carry on, but it wasn't much fun, anymore. Jason tried his best to make a special effort and always gave us a cherished gift by cooking us a gourmet meal every Christmas Eve. Cooking is definitely a gift of love and every year, I couldn't wait to see what he had in store for us. It became my favourite part of Christmas.

When Jason's Grandma Grace was diagnosed with lymphoma, he became very concerned. He wanted pictures of Grandma and Papa when they were young and couldn't bear the thought of them getting old. He was still having trouble with the subject of death. I, too, worried about my parents. Since I was an only child, I was very close to them.

Jay fell in love with a girl named April. On their wedding day, our old house came alive once more, as the entire wedding party got ready there.

At one point, Jason rang my Grandfather's old cow bell.

"Groom coming upstairs," he yelled, to warn the girls. He and April got married in our front yard, under a trellis that Bill and I had made for them. The lake provided a beautiful backdrop while the guests watched the ceremony.

I liked his wife and was really happy for them, but unfortunately the marriage didn't last. When they split up, Jay wrote April a song saying that she had a wonderful smile and he wanted her to find happiness so that beautiful smile would shine through again. I wanted that for April, too.

Life seemed to go on, but I began to worry about Jason. I thought that he might be depressed because he seemed to be sleeping a lot during the day and staying up at night. I teased him about it, saying that I was afraid he was becoming a mole. I wanted him to get more sunshine.

The Christmas before Jay was diagnosed with cancer, he gave us a second gift. Grandma and Papa usually sang, and Jason and Papa played guitar, but that year Jay called us into the family room and sang us the old blues song *Don't Cry for Me (When I'm Gone)*. At the end of the song, he picked out *Amazing Grace* for his Grandma Grace. We were all shocked, but overjoyed, when he actually sang the words.

Over Christmas dinner, he mentioned that he had been having a lot of pain deep inside on his upper side. The doctor thought it was from playing the guitar for hours and working on the assembly line at work. Physiotherapy didn't seem to be helping.

Shortly after Christmas, he phoned me from the city and said that he had coughed up some blood while he was singing. He had looked up all his symptoms on the Internet; he was sure he had tuberculosis. I told him that it was highly unlikely, but he should come into the office, first thing Monday morning, and I would ask if Dr. Kent would do a chest x-ray, and TB skin test. Jason's TB test was negative, but his x-ray came back showing pneumonia. We were both relieved that antibiotics would fix him up.

Two weeks later, however, Jason's new x-ray still showed pneumonia. We sent him for a CT scan around 11 a.m. and Dr. Kent had just left for lunch, when I received the imaging phone report about Jason. I was in disbelief as I wrote down the mind-blowing diagnosis: a tumour, a missing rib and lung invasion that looked like cancer. A voice inside my head was screaming, "No, this can't be happening. Not Jason. Not my son."

The x-ray technician never knew that he was giving the report to the patient's mother. In sheer panic, I called Dr. Kent at home and gave him the news. He said there had to be some mistake and that he was heading to the hospital imaging department right away. A few minutes later he came into the office with a very worried look on his face. He said we had to make some calls to a thoracic surgeon to get Jason in for some more tests. He wanted the other girls to handle it, but I refused. I felt so helpless; I had to do everything in my power to speed things along, to help my son.

Poor Jason. When he got the news that it was lung cancer, and it sank in, he said, "Now, I have to face my greatest fear."

Life as we knew it changed, once again. Everything moved along very quickly. We didn't have a chance to think too much. In order to cope, I made up imaginary boxes for myself. I would only allow one thing in the box at a time. If Jason had an appointment with a surgeon,

I put that appointment in a box and wouldn't look beyond. When we had dealt with that appointment, I would make another imaginary box for the next test or procedure. It was my way of staying in control, not looking too far ahead, and just dealing with the moment at hand, instead of thinking of all the what-ifs. Jason needed me to be strong for him. One day I mentioned to Sal that I was thinking about selling our house to move to town to be closer to Jay and the hospital. I also came up with a few more brilliant plans to try to fix the situation.

"Jude," she said. "Get back in your box. You're talking crazy."

We could never mention the possibility of Jason dying because he couldn't go there. He would only talk about finding cures. He started looking at every possibility. As much as I wanted to believe Jason would be cured, deep down inside I knew that his destiny had already been written.

As a part of my journey, I began reading books on the subject of coping. Some people say there is power in knowledge. Lance Armstrong's book gave me hope since he beat all the odds. In one of Elisabeth Kubler-Ross' books, she writes about being depressed when she took a position at a children's cancer ward. She couldn't believe how these young children, who were deep in adversity, could smile like angels, showing wisdom and compassion beyond their years. These children were an inspiration and lifted her spirits.

Bernie Siegel's book *Love, Medicine, and Miracles* was also helpful and uplifting. He tells the story about a man who was bedridden, with only a few weeks to live. The man had heard about an experimental drug and begged to be allowed to try it. Because his cancer was so advanced, his request was refused. Somehow, he convinced the doctors to make an exception and allow him to become part of the study. Miraculously, he improved to the point where he was able to live a normal life. He even flew his plane again. A few months later, he read in a newspaper that his drug trials had failed. His condition immediately began to deteriorate and he died shortly after. That story really showed the power of mind over body. I think Jason showed a lot of this during his illness.

Within a couple of weeks, Jay had lung biopsies and lung surgery in Newmarket and then he was sent to The Princess Margaret Hospital in Toronto, by ambulance, for more tests. I rode down in the ambulance with him. On the way back to Newmarket, the nurse in the ambulance started getting carsick. Jason told her to ride in the front seat. He said he was fine with me. We were two tough nuts.

We had an appointment at the Princess Margaret to discuss chemotherapy. I remember sitting in the doctor's tiny office, listening to our options, and hearing the bad news. She said that in a normal year the hospital saw very few cases like Jason's.

My son sat on the examining table and I sat behind the doctor, facing him. As we listened to the heart-wrenching news, I had trouble keeping my composure. As the doctor talked, she noticed that Jason wasn't concentrating. Instead he was staring at me. The doctor rolled her stool back, so she could rest her hand on my knee and continued. Later when this doctor's report came back to my doctor's office, I read what it said. The doctor said that any boy who showed more concern about his mother than himself was truly commendable. After that appointment, Jason would not allow me to attend his appointments.

One day I went into Jason's bathroom and saw this saying taped to his mirror:

When it is darkest,
Men see the stars.

RALPH WALDO EMERSON

The hospital set up chemo for the following week. Once again, my friend BF came through for me. He often drove me to Toronto and let me stay at his friend Terry's condo, which was within walking distance of the Princess Margaret. Jason either stayed at the Princess Margaret lodge, or with friends.

The doctors at the clinic where I worked were very supportive, allowing me to take off whatever time I needed. I valued the time Jay and I spent in the city. We found Baldwin Street, with its unique restaurants, behind the Princess Margaret and would try different culinary experiences including Mexican, Italian and Indian. When Jason got tired between treatments, we would sometimes go to a movie matinee. I wanted to spend as much time with him as I could. I knew that our time was precious.

Jason began to change. He started pushing me away. One time, I knew he had a chemo appointment on a Friday, so I took the bus down to Toronto and walked over to the Princess Margaret from the bus station to surprise him. I arrived just as he was going into his appointment. He was furious with me.

"What are you doing here?" he asked. "I said I didn't need you. You can just turn around and go back home because I have plans this weekend."

He did come over to the condo for a while, but he was very distant and then he left. When he was gone, I felt broken and alone. I had come all this way hoping to spend just a bit of quality time with my son and it was all for nothing. I had been dismissed. I very seldom cry, but at that moment, I broke down.

Jason's quote:

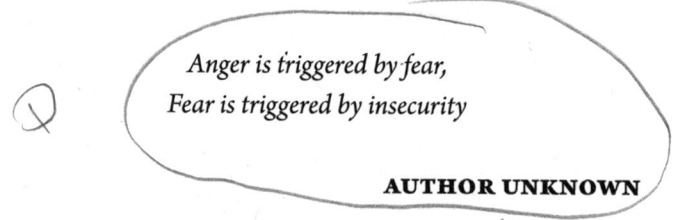

Anger is triggered by fear,
Fear is triggered by insecurity

AUTHOR UNKNOWN

BF tried to cheer me up by taking me for a walk to Union Station and up Yonge Street. He pointed out the Pantages Theatre and told the story of how workers discovered the hidden Winter Garden Theatre when they did a renovation. He's an engineer and he showed me some of the city architecture, in places where I probably wouldn't have noticed them on my own. It was good to have a friend at that moment. Unfortunately, he couldn't stay long because he had plans to take the train out of town for the weekend. A couple of hours later, I was saying good-bye to BF at Union Station and was left alone once more in the big city. I thought I would make the best of it and headed back up Yonge Street.

I went into the Eaton's Centre and got even more depressed when every piece of clothing I looked at seemed to be designed for skinny models. I phoned a girlfriend to see if she wanted to meet me for dinner, but it was too late, and she had made plans. I was just saying good-bye to the friend, when I saw my cousin, two floors below, in the courtyard. I yelled at the top of my voice.

"N-A-N-C-Y!"

She seemed confused, looked around, until she saw me waving from the balcony, and yelled back.

"JUDY! What are you doing here?"

I hadn't seen her for ages. It turned out that she had driven in from Acton to meet a girlfriend to see Martin Short at the Pantages Theatre. The first thing we did was head to a Laura store which sells plus-sized clothing. Immediately, I started to feel better. We had a quick supper before the performance. I decided to walk them over to the theatre to see if there was a ticket available close enough to join them. Sure enough, I got a seat in close proximity to them. Martin worked his magic and had us in stitches for the whole performance. Nancy dropped me off at the condo on her way back to Acton.

What were the chances of running into her? Someone must have been looking after me that night. I had a great story to tell Jason so that neither one of us would feel guilty. I told BF that I got to see inside of the Pantages Theatre, the very theatre he had shown me that afternoon. Something bad turned into a great day. I'm glad that I didn't choose the feeling-sorry-for-myself road; to stay in the condo alone and miserable. Everyone would have lost.

A while later, Jay and I finally had a heart-to-heart. I told him to talk to me, that nothing he would say could hurt me more than him pushing me away. I told him how much I loved him and that I just wanted to be there for him. He explained that he was fighting the battle of his life and he had to feel strong. When I was around, it made him feel sick, weak and vulnerable. He couldn't concentrate if I went to his appointments with him. He might want to get angry, or swear, but he was on his guard when I was there because he didn't want to upset me. I understood and wished that we had had that conversation earlier. We made a truce. I could come to some appointments, if I waited in the waiting room and agreed not to ask him any questions and pretend that everything was normal. I later heard from one of Jason's close friends that he was trying to protect me because he knew what I had gone through after Mark died.

My dear, brave-hearted son.

Jay was a very private person, but as a friend, he was also very loyal. I didn't realize how many friends he had until he got sick. They planned two fundraisers to help with expenses, especially so that Jay could afford some special medication. Both fundraisers had local bands playing and were very well attended. Unfortunately, the first one was held just after Jay had received chemo and he was supposed to stay away from crowds. When I went down to meet him at the Princess Margaret, the next Friday, I couldn't believe how sick he was. He looked like a little old man waiting for me outside the hospital. I helped him walk over to the condo, which we had to ourselves because Terry and BF were in Europe. He never complained, but I knew he was very sick. He had to spend most of the weekend in bed until the antibiotics began to kick in.

It was around this time that Jay began seeing Sarah. It was a hard decision for her to start a relationship with someone who was so ill, but she decided that it was worth it. Once they started dating, they became inseparable and began working on Jason's cure together. Every time I went to see them, they would be sitting on the couch checking out Internet sites for healthy food choices and different vitamins and herbs.

They were good for each other. There were always encouraging notes on their fridge, things like "It's a good day, be happy," or "Never give up." One morning Sarah woke up, after Jason had gone out and found the following note on her pillow:

I'm yesterday's memories,
Today's love,
And tomorrow's dreams.

I was shocked when Jason and I had a lunch date and he mentioned that he was reading a book that Sarah had given him.

"Don't get upset, Mom," he explained. "But it is about a guy who is dying who appreciates every day."

I asked him if it was *Tuesdays with Morrie*, by Mitch Albom and he seemed surprised that his mom would have read this book. Actually, I loved the book and thought it might help Jason, but didn't have the nerve to give it to him. I knew if I had suggested that he read it, he probably would have been upset with me. It amazed me that Sarah had the same idea and was able to introduce it to Jay in a way that would help with his journey.

For the moment, life seemed to be going pretty well and they both seemed very happy. Jason called Sarah his muse. He surprised us with an announcement, just before Christmas, that he and Sarah were going to Italy and Spain for three weeks in May. Dr. Kent agreed a holiday would be good for him but suggested that they might want to choose an earlier date and consider someplace closer in Canada. But as I've said, when Jason made his mind up, there was no changing it. He insisted that they were going in May and that was final. All we could do was wish them well and help them out financially. Jay didn't have any insurance coverage. I knew that his condition meant that his spine could give out at any time. If the cancer hit a vital organ, he would also be in trouble. I made sure my own passport was up to date in case I had to fly over to be with them.

By the time May came, Dr. Kent wished Jay well. He also made him promise not to do anything foolish. We all held our breath and sent them on their way with love and a prayer. Sarah set up a blog. At work every day, everyone would gather around my desk and we would all read what was happening in Italy. It sounded as if they were having a wonderful time. Jason, who had never had a sweet tooth, had developed a taste for gelato. Since he was such a good cook, he enjoyed trying the Italian cuisine at the authentic little bistros and restaurants. One evening, they were having a special meal when an accordion player came over to their table and began singing.

"K Sarah, Sarah, Whatever will be, will be. The answer's not ours to see, K Sarah, Sarah."

Sarah was sure that he was singing to her, and couldn't figure out how he knew her name. We didn't have the heart to tell her he was singing, "Que sera, sera."

One morning when I opened the blog, I read Jay's announcement that he had climbed the 463 stairs in the Duomo of the Cattedrale di Santa Maria del Fiore in Florence. We couldn't believe it because, by then, Jay only had about a half a lung working properly. He had lost one rib and part of another one to this terrible disease. After reading this announcement, Dr. Kent had to go into his office to have a moment alone.

It made my day, one Saturday, when I picked up the phone and heard,

"Buongiorno!" on the other end of the line. Jay sounded so happy and excited; it was wonderful to hear his voice. He said that he was feeling well but they were pacing themselves because he did get very tired. He hoped that I didn't mind that he had spent some extra money and bought a guitar at the market. He was missing his music. How could I mind? I was so thankful and pleased that he was having a good time. He mentioned that he was a bit worried because his stomach was bloating. I told him that it was probably his liver acting up.

The next call we got was from the airport. They were safely on the ground and wanted all of us – me and Bill and Grandma and Papa – to meet Sarah's Mom and Grandmother at Sarah's condo for a welcome home dinner the next day. Jason was going to cook us an Italian and

Spanish meal. They had bought a new barbeque on the way home that Sarah was trying to put together when we arrived. Papa immediately joined in to help her. It was a perfect evening. We started out with sangria and bruschetta, followed by a wonderful paella with fruit for dessert. Jay and Sarah showed us their pictures on their television, then Jason made an announcement that they were going to have a celebration of their love on our dock in August. They were elated and so was everyone who attended. It had been a miracle that they were home safe and that their trip had gone so well. I have no idea how Jay had the energy to cook such a meal after making the long journey home.

Unfortunately, shortly after the trip, Jay began to go downhill quickly. He and Dr. Kent had agreed that Jay would run his own show. As the song says, "He did it his way." One day I got a call at work that he needed oxygen because he was having trouble breathing; it was arranged the same day. I would stop in to bring him soup, or he would call when he needed something. As he got weaker, I packed my bag hoping that he would let me stay, but I was always sent back home. One night, I came to deliver a walker to him, and found him in bad shape. Sarah was working and didn't realize how bad he really was. They always felt that he would get better and they would be together.

"I guess you might as well stay," Jay said.

I never left.

Grandma and Papa and I purchased a La-Z-Boy reclining chair for Jay because he didn't want to have a hospital bed. Sarah, Jay and I all slept in the living room because he could no longer climb the stairs to the bedroom. Jay asked if I would mind sleeping on the love seat, so Sarah could have the couch. Of course I didn't mind; I just needed to be there.

One day when I asked him what he would like to eat, he answered, "Eggs Benedict." He thought that I should learn to make hollandaise sauce from scratch. He looked up a recipe on his computer. He read out what I was supposed to be doing, from his command seat in the La-Z-Boy and I would respond "Check," "Roger," and so on. Once he realized that we were ahead, or behind, in making the recipe from his instructions, he tried to stir the bowl on his lap, while I made the next stage. I must say our giant bowl of hollandaise sauce turned out amazingly well. Jay could only manage a couple of bites, but the most important thing was the memory that we made it together.

The La-Z-Boy didn't work for long, so the time came to get a hospital bed. Bill and his buddies, Rob and Carlo, came by to move the La-Z-Boy to my Mom and Dad's house to make room for the bed. Carlo was completely natural with Jay and was able to joke with him, but Rob had trouble dealing with his illness. I can still picture him standing at the top of the living room stairs, with tears in his eyes. Jay wasn't as upset as he thought he would be, when he moved to the hospital bed, because we put it next to the couch where he could be close to Sarah.

Jason's good friend, Al, came to visit and played the guitar for a while. He was very relaxed and helped me turn Jay on the bed. He said that he used to look after his father so he was comfortable dealing with illness. He brought a sense of calm with him.

Jay sent out an email to his buddies saying that he was sorry he hadn't been in touch; they must think he was a real jerk. He wrote that he was really sick, right now, but if they could only give him two weeks, he would be well enough to make it up to them. I guess the word spread that Jay wasn't doing well. That night, about a dozen of his friends showed up, gathering around his hospital bed, sharing stories about their adventures with Jay. He couldn't speak very much.

"I thought I told you to leave me alone for two weeks," Jay said.

"When have we ever paid any attention to you, Snoddon?" they chimed in together.

It was heart-warming and heart-wrenching at the same time.

The next day, Jay's friend Eric brought a picture of "Jason (from England), Eric and Jay," to show Jay. Jay smiled and weakly whispered, "The Three Musketeers." That was all he could say. Eric said he was thankful for that moment.

Grandma and Papa came to say goodbye. Papa was upset because he thought Jason didn't know him. He didn't realize that Jason didn't have the strength to speak. As his Papa turned to leave, Jay made a kissing sound – neither of my boys ever missed kissing their grandparents when they said goodbye. I told my Dad, "Of course, he knows you because he just gave you a kiss."

The next day, Jay was gone. He died with his two cats at the foot of his bed and his mother kneeling by his side. Sarah was kneeling on the other side to help him complete his journey. When he looked scared, she cupped his face in her hands.

"Look into my eyes, darling," Sarah said. "Everything will be fine, just look into my eyes."

She just knew the right thing to do, while I let him down by fretting and worrying at the last moment, trying too hard to help him instead of just being there for him. Sarah was his Angel, sent to help him face his greatest fear.

By this time, Dr. Kent was kneeling beside us as well. Death is not like it is in the movies. When the spirit of life leaves the body, it seems like such an empty vessel. When the reality of the situation sank in for Sarah, she immediately went inside herself. She was like a frightened lost soul.

"It wasn't supposed to end this way," she said.

I took her in my arms and told her that she and Jason had a love that some people never experience. We would always be eternally grateful that she came into his life to help with his journey. She ran to the comfort of friends.

I waited until they took Jay away and then instinctively removed all the drugs and bedding. I took one final look around, threw my things together, than began the long drive home. Looking back, I don't even remember how many days I stayed with Jay and Sarah. The time flowed together in an endless stream of sleepless nights and days. I just knew that I was where I needed to be.

Bill and our Lake of Bays' family were waiting for me when I arrived home after eleven. I hugged everyone, explaining the night's events.

I couldn't cry. I guess it would have taken too much energy and I didn't have anything left to give.

The next day, Sarah went out and got a tattoo around her wrist, like an eternity bracelet.

It read: "I'm yesterday's memories, today's love and tomorrow's dreams."

It was the special gift that Jay had left for her alone. No one could take that away from her. I found myself thinking about the saying, "It is better to have loved and lost, than never to have loved at all."

Jason never complained and fought his journey with true grit, class and bravery. He will always be a true superhero to me.

There must be a reason before I was born, you had
written in your book everything I would do.

PSALM 139:16

A couple of days after Jay passed, we had all of his buddies out to the house for a barbeque. We planned what songs they would play for the funeral. I asked if anyone had a copy of the CD Jason had made with the song *Don't Cry for Me (When I'm Gone)*. No one knew what I was talking about. They said they had never heard him sing that song. I knew it existed because Jason had played it for me. It was a mystery.

Jason had about twelve guitars and his only wish was that his buddies each have one. He said they would know who would get which one. They all went home with their guitars that night.

I went on a mission to find Jason's song. It started at Shawn's house, where Jason had done a lot of taping. Shawn wasn't aware of the CD, but, when I was leaning on the island in his Mother's kitchen, I noticed a CD sitting on the counter that I recognized. It was the one Jason had played for me. Shawn's mom handed me the CD with a bewildered, questioning shrug. Neither one of us knew why it was there, but I was certainly glad to find it.

The next day, Bill and I were stretched out on lounge chairs on the veranda. Bill was dozing while I was trying to write a eulogy for

Jay entitled "Facing our Fears". All at once, a silly rabbit came hopping up the veranda steps and went right under our lounges. He hopped to the other end of the veranda, but it was too high up for him to jump off. Confused, he hopped back over to Bill and me, paused in front of us, and looked up with an expression that seemed to say, "Well, this was a dumb move. What do I do now?" He then found his way back to where he came from and went on his way. It wasn't a little buck deer, but it was a nice little visit and a bit of a diversion. Some of Jay's friends used to call him Tigger because he was always hopping from one place to another.

Like Mark, Jason also had a large funeral. We had to rent the fairgrounds to fit everyone in. Several of his buddies played their guitars and wore sunglasses, which was one of Jay's signature looks. His friend Jason, who was like a brother, flew home from England to attend the funeral. Several people spoke and shared their special memories. In closing, we presented a slideshow of his life, with the CD of Jason singing *Don't Cry for Me (When I'm Gone)* in the background. At the end of the song he picked out *Amazing Grace*, for his grandma, like he had done at Christmas.

*****

A couple of days after the funeral, I thought about how supportive my clinic doctors had been during Jason's illness. To show our appreciation, we invited them and their wives for a barbeque on our dock. As a surprise, after the main course, I had Lake of Bays Boat Tour arrive to take everyone on an evening cruise to Dorset for an ice cream cone. It was a nice relaxing diversion after the grief and turmoil of the weeks and months before. Our captain, Bruce, had thoughtfully added warm drinks and a bouquet of flowers in Jason's honour. The weather co-operated and on the way home as we approached the end of Bigwin Island, a beautiful sunset filled the sky. Bruce anchored the boat and I distributed the flowers to our guests. In the atmosphere of this special moment, I read Raichel's poem of "Jason sitting on a star, playing his guitar". While the sun slowly disappeared and the calm and stillness of evening surrounded us, we felt a soothing sense of peace. We all took a moment to pause and reflect on the memory of Jason, before we tossed our flowers into the still water. As the boat slowly returned to shore, we all sensed the euphoric moment that we had shared.

*****

When a person we love dies of cancer, it is so different from a suicide death. We have time to accept things and brace ourselves for that sudden jolt at the end. When we see someone we love suffering from such an illness, we are ready to let that person go, to let them find peace. I think we start mourning the minute they are diagnosed.

As life went on, I took a little side trip down the "poor me" road. Gardening lost its magic and became a chore. Joy didn't come very often and junk food became my friend. This time, I began to spend money and shopped too much. I must have been searching for another kind of happiness. Money didn't mean anything anymore, since I didn't have the boys to leave it to. I was trying to make myself feel better by buying new clothes and senseless, material things. Looking back, I know now that it was another version of depression rearing its ugly head.

I felt extremely worn out. I had to push myself to keep up with my work at home and at the clinic. It was important to me to do a good job, to keep up a happy face, to go that extra mile for my patients and fellow workers. It was important to me to make my work matter, to make a difference in the one world over which I had some control.

One night, I was so exhausted on the way home from work that I didn't think I would make it all the way. Suddenly, a dark shadow emerged from the back seat of the car and encircled me. It wasn't frightening – instead I felt a calm come over me. I felt a boost of energy that allowed me to drive home safely. I don't think it was Jason, but something certainly gave me a helping hand that night. Maybe it was my Guardian Angel.

Once again, thanks to all my support systems and lessons, I soon got back on the road to recovery. Remembering the poem *To All Parents* (see page 132) I knew that we were fortunate to have had the boys in our lives, even though it wasn't for long enough.

Jason's friend from England – also named Jason – had a hard time dealing with losing Jay. He carried his picture around for ages. He watched the video of the funeral so many times that his father-in-law took it away because he thought his obsession with it was unhealthy. One night, Jason heard his little girl talking in her room. He went in to see if she was alright. She said she was fine and told him she was just talking to Snoddon, who was sitting in the chair by her bed. Her Dad told her there was no one there, and then settled her back to sleep. A couple of days later, after finishing a swimming lesson, she was on her way to the change room.

"Goodbye, Snoddon." she said.

Her mother asked her what she was talking about, and she explained that Jay had been watching her swim. That was the last time she saw him. It makes me happy to think that Jay was free, and in a better place. I guess he stopped in England to say goodbye and to let everyone know he was fine and not afraid anymore.

All of the boys' friends kept tabs on us and came by for several Christmas get-togethers. Bill and I hired a bus to bring them out to the house and I cooked them dinner. The boys brought their guitars and played us some music. I was never happier than when the house was bursting at the seams with young people having a good time. They would tell me stories all night of Jason and Mark's antics. I couldn't believe some of the stories. At one point, we had seven guitars playing at once in the family room. It was great! One year Geordie brought his bagpipes; the family room walls shook that night.

Those gatherings got Bill and me through the first few Christmases after losing the boys. We are so thankful that everyone cared enough to make the trip. On the first Christmas gathering after losing Jay, my boys from the Acrimony band gave me a dog-tag necklace with Jay's picture sketched on both sides. They said they wanted to get Mark's picture sketched on it as well, but didn't have a picture of him. I was truly touched. I had lost my boys, but I was blessed to have so many of Jay and Mark's friends in my life.

The next year, I went to a dance recital to watch our niece. I was sitting in the audience waiting for the program to begin, when all of a sudden the stage was filled with a full-sized picture of Jay. A voice came over the PA system.

"This performance is dedicated to my good friend, Jason Snoddon. Thank you, Jay, for believing in me and encouraging me to follow my dream."

I was overcome with surprise, pride, curiosity, and joy.

After the show, I made a point of going down to meet the curator and owner of the studio, Wendy Laidlaw. She told me that she had become discouraged with teaching dance and didn't enjoy working at a particular studio. Jay came to watch some of her student's rehearsals. Sometimes he brought a piece of music that he thought might work for her choreography. She said that she would never have picked out some of those pieces, but to her surprise, they worked.

She had decided to quit, but Jason said she had too much talent to throw away. He encouraged her to open her own studio, to do it her way. She now operates a very successful dance studio called Just 4 Kicks. Several of her students have won prestigious awards. Thank you, Wendy, for acknowledging Jay and for making a difference by moulding so many young students into better people. Your studio gives them confidence in themselves, improves their balance and poise and makes them more well-rounded individuals. You have also made a difference in my life by letting me know that Jay had a small part in making this happen.

At work one day, a girl asked me if I was Jason Snoddon's mother. She said she had known Jason in high school. Apparently, she had had a bit of a reputation then and when she walked by a group of boys, they began to taunt her. She felt totally humiliated, embarrassed and cheap. Jason stepped out from the group and defended her, giving the boys a hard time. He walked her down the hallway to get away from the situation. She told me that she would always be thankful to him for being a gentleman and for giving her back some dignity. I let her know how much I appreciated her telling me this story.

I recently dug out a little red diary I had used to write down some quotes over the years – I thought it might be useful with my writing. Sadly, this was a journal that I had planned to leave for my boys to read after I died, hoping that it would help them in life. It upset me to read it after their passing, because children aren't supposed to die before their parents. It also upset me because I had told them that I was worried they weren't being responsible with their finances, that I was worried about their future. It really upset the boys when I brought up the subject of money. After losing them, it seemed so petty of me. I felt guilty for making such a big deal out of something so unimportant now. I wished that I could have a chance to make it up to them.

As I was looking through the different messages, a small card fell out on my lap. It was from a day long before Jason's illness when, out of the blue, he had flowers delivered to me at work with a card attached that read, "To the kindest woman I know, Love Jayson." It was the best gift and compliment that I could ever receive from my son. The flowers are long gone, but I will treasure this little card for the rest of my life. Jason was right – he was a healer.

You might wonder why Jason is spelled in so many different ways in this book. When Jay was born we named him Jason, which was often shortened to Jay. Because Jason wanted to be unique, he always signed his name, Jayson. All spellings work for me.

Jason's friends also encircled Sarah with support and encouragement. She ended up marrying a member of the Acrimony band and Bill and I had the honour of being invited to their wedding. Their little family is doing well.

Have We Been Led Down the Wrong Path?

Jason wrote this piece when he was first diagnosed with cancer:

It all began when, after performing,
I thought I'd injured my back by playing my guitar behind my head.
After many months of therapy, with no results, my doctor ordered a CT scan.
That's when all hell broke loose.
The word tumour first, which evolved into cancer.
When you are sitting in a clinic, medical professionals telling you awful things,
"The world stops."
You quickly realize that under the wings of life, we are all equal.
We have only life, death, health, and sickness.
All the plans of retirement, buying a new car, acquiring material things,
It all goes out the window.
I never asked, "Why me?" because disease is unprejudiced. We have no control!

But what I do question are the things we do have control over. We have allowed society, government, corporations, and people with guided ideals to choose our paths and lifestyle.

This large wheel keeps spinning, getting bigger, and moving faster. Our lifestyles are more rushed than ever – paying bills, working too many hours, never getting ahead.

Watching television instead of a starry night or a sunset.

Are children getting less attention and learning from us, that this way of life is acceptable?

Is it acceptable? I'll say it, "Know! It's not!"

People need to start taking life by the moment. Do the things that make them happy, follow their dreams and passions instead of the media and advertising community's vision.

Life has to be simple, with fewer products, wasting less, using less, and wanting less. I truly believe our lifestyle is the biggest health issue on the planet.

There is no love put into cooking a McDonald's burger. The only concern is the bottom line. Life should not follow this train of thought. It is unnatural to our survival. We have become dependent on grocery and fast food corporations. What will happen when, say, the bird flu strikes and all the trucks that deliver food to our local destinations stop? Then what? Most have lost the agrarian knowledge of planting a garden, making preserves, keeping hens. Our rushed lifestyles make little or no time for gardening etc……So people will starve or steal to survive.

This seems crazy!!!

Because generations before us lived this way – off the land. This makes my point.

We have been led down the wrong path.

Since my sickness was discovered, I now notice little things. I appreciate small moments. Most of which cost nothing – and are found everywhere – in nature and people. I take the time to smell the roses.

To most in the rat race these gifts go unnoticed. Their attention spans have been stolen. Be it by video games, cell phones, advertising, or movies. They suck you in. They are designed to win.

Our freedom, health, future, and survival are a deck of cards thrown in the air. We need to ask ourselves "What if it is me tomorrow sitting in a cancer ward?"

On a long enough timeline, we all run out of time. Tomorrow is promised to no one.

So let's start a movement to slow things down. Take our lives back!

Encourage our towns, communities, and governments that this change is vital for each human's wellbeing and balance. Focus on living free. Spend quality time with our families and friends, working together, being self-sufficient, growing fresh vegetables and producing our own products. Spend less time depending on a system that is destroying our world and taking us farther from the righteous path.

A moment in the mind of Jayson Snoddon

2007

Poems

I read this poem when we buried Jason's ashes. Thank you, Raichel, for this special gift from your heart.

Looking out the window,
You're all over the sky
Dancing on the wind and learning how to fly.
You left this dimension but not without extension
From us to you above.
Never without love
From people that you love
And friends who watched you grow.
Every day with show
The person that you were,
The entity you are,
Sitting on a star,
Strumming your guitar.
Forever in your hands,
Exploring foreign lands
In your white suit,
To you we salute
And are looking forward to
The day that we see you
And get to know the truth.
When it is our turn
To learn all you have learned
And the wings that you have earned

Jason

We know it's not the end
And we just wonder when
We'll see you again.
Mom, Dad, and all your friends,
Your family, we send
Wishes, joy, and fun
To Jayson, number one.
You opened up the door to the other side with a brave stride and
Even though we cried
You were outfitted with wings and now an angel sings
From the bottom of the earth – into the universe.
His cells are in the stars,
He goes on trips to Mars.
He doesn't need a car
To get from near to far.
It's all within his reach
And one fine day he'll teach
Us how to walk the clouds
And ride on waves of sound
With feet above the ground.
He's always to be found,
He'll always be around,
Living it out loud,
Laughing up a storm with babies b4 they're born.
Travelling in time – not waiting in lines,
Health repaired, restored,
He'll strike another chord.
The orchestra will play
Each and every day
He's visiting.

Love, (+by)

Raichel Mariko Balzereit

One of Jason's co-workers, Jamie Hudson, from the Dura plant, drew his rendition of Jason and brought several copies to the funeral. It suits our dream of Jay, floating on a star playing his guitar. A few weeks later, my sister Cathy's husband, Mike, took his copy to a gallery to have it framed and matted. He felt it deserved to be treated with dignity. Mike and Cathy presented the finished product to Bill and me. It now hangs with Mark's picture in our bedroom. Can't you feel the love of people caring for other people? One good deed leads to another.

I found it intriguing that both Jamie and Raichel had the same concept of Jason sitting on a star playing his guitar and they both brought them as gifts to the funeral. They didn't know each other, but they obviously knew Jason.

The following poem was given to us by friends a few months after we lost Mark. It gave me a new way of looking at losing a child. I hope it helps you as well. I have changed the ages to those of Mark and Jason.

To All Parents

I'll lend you for a little time a child of mine, He said,
For you to love him while he lives, and mourn for when he's dead.
It may be six or seven years, or twenty-two or thirty-three,
But will you, 'til I call him back, take care of him for me?
He'll bring his charms to gladden you, and shall his stay be brief,
You'll have his lovely memories as solace for your grief.
I cannot promise he will stay, since all from Earth return,
But there are lessons taught down there, I want this child to learn.
I've looked the wide world over in my search for teachers true
And from the throngs that crowd life's lanes, I have selected you.
Now, will you give him all your love, not think the labour vain,
Nor hate me when I come to call to take him back again?
I fancied that I heard them say, dear Lord, Thy will be done!
For all the joy Thy child shall bring, the risk of grief we'll run.
We'll shelter him with tenderness; we'll love him while we may,
And for the happiness we've known, forever grateful stay.
But shall the angels call for him much sooner than we've planned,

We'll brave the bitter grief that comes and try
to understand.

EDGAR GUEST

Pilgrimage to Florence

The miracle of Jay walking up the 463 stairs, in the Duomo in Florence, had a real effect on Dr. Kent and me. While he was visiting Europe, Dr. Kent decided to make a side trip to Florence to climb Jason's stairs. When they were about three-quarters of the way up, his wife said it was almost too difficult for her. When she realized that Jay had completed his journey in terrible health, she regained her strength and made it to the top. Because it was so difficult, she was even more aware of the miracle, and the wonder of Jason's willpower.

That evening, Dr. Kent took a stroll by himself, through the narrow streets of Florence, to reflect on the events that unfolded both that day and during Jason's illness. When he came to a courtyard where people often gathered to sit by the fountain, he saw a young couple singing. He was drawn to their music and their appearance. The boy, playing his guitar, truly resembled Jay. His partner, who was happily dancing and singing to the music, looked just like Sarah. They looked so content and joyful as they followed their dream by entertaining people for a little extra money.

Dr. Kent had been looking for a sign from Jay and this was it. He bought the young couple's CD and gave it to me as a souvenir from their trip. It was perfect. I listened to it every day on the way to work and wished that Jay and Sarah were following their dreams as well.

When I turned sixty, it was my turn to climb the Duomo, in Florence. A group of B & B owners were taking a trip to Italy and

Florence was on their itinerary. At the last minute, one couple dropped out because of health problems so my girlfriend Sue and I took their place. We had flown in by ourselves, and made plans to meet the group in Florence, where we would stay with one of the couples, in a small apartment. We found our way there and met up with everyone in time to have dinner at one of the many *ristorantes*. The next day, I couldn't wait to explore the city to feel what Jason and Sarah had felt. Everyone had made their own separate plans, so Sue and I decided to go off on our own and meet the others that evening to exchange stories of the day's adventures.

The first thing on our list was finding the Duomo. We didn't think that it would be that difficult because, when we arrived in the city, we could see its silhouette towering over the terracotta-roofed buildings from every angle. We began walking down the narrow cobblestoned streets in what we hoped was the right direction. Florence is like a maze of ancient buildings, bistros, delicious smells, colourful flower-pots, as well as leather and clothing shops. Many of the shopkeepers stood outside coaxing us to come in. Motor scooters buzzed around us, as we walked along, looking from side to side, and up and down, with wide curious eyes. We were drinking in all the wonders of the magnificent city. Every once in a while, we would get a glimpse of the Duomo peaking around a corner, or pick out its curved roof top above the buildings. At that moment I felt truly happy.

Sue was a good companion to share this experience. We had been married one week apart, by the same minister, and our boys, Jason and Adam, had been in the same hospital nursery when they were born. Mark and Sue's son Luke were also close in age. As mothers of sons, and true adventurers, we both felt the wonder and passion of Italy. In our search for the Duomo, we seemed to be walking in circles. We decided to stop at a café to have a glass of wine. We wanted to celebrate the fact that we were there and just take a moment to soak up the experience of Florence. It was great to blend in and feel like locals, as we watched everyone go about their daily business. When we got the bill, however, we didn't feel like locals at all – our glasses of wine cost fifteen Euros each! When we questioned it, the waitress said there was a surcharge for sitting on the patio. Apparently, it's cheaper to stand at the bar.

After our little refreshment, we successfully made it to the famous Piazza del Duomo, the plaza in front of the awe-inspiring cathedral. It was the hub of Florence, with entertainment, fountains and other impressive buildings. I couldn't help but notice that there is very little grass in Florence – it's almost entirely paved with cobblestones and cement.

I had heard that there were long lineups to climb the Duomo stairs and that first thing in the morning was the best time to make the climb. While we were getting our bearings, we saw a sign that we thought was the entrance to the Duomo and to our surprise, there wasn't a lineup. I hugged Sue and we bought a ticket to go in. There was a small museum on the ground floor, where we stopped for a quick look, but I was anxious to begin our ascent. This was it. My moment had finally arrived. We slowly started climbing the stairs and found, on the third-storey landing, an open window that looked out onto the courtyard. Sue and I walked over to the window to admire the view. There, right in front of us, was the Duomo, nearly taking up the entire view. We couldn't believe our eyes and immediately snapped the Duomo picture that appears at the beginning of this section.

It turns out, we weren't in the Duomo. We were in the Baptistry of Saint John, a smaller, older, building in front of the main cathedral. We burst out laughing. It could only happen to us!

We finally found the real entrance to the Duomo where there was, indeed, a long lineup. We made plans to come back first thing the next morning to carry out our mission. We spent the day exploring the banks of the Arno River and the Ponte Vecchio, which was built in 1218. This ancient arched bridge was wide enough to have a whole street of shops built along both sides of its entire length. There were expensive jewelry and clothing shops, art galleries and the famous gelato booths. Of course, Sue and I had to indulge in Jason's gelato. He was right; it had such real fruit flavour and it didn't seem as heavy or filling as Canadian ice cream.

We seemed to have walked for miles. In true Judy and Sue style (or Ethel and Lucy style, since those were our new nicknames), we got lost. We asked someone if they could tell us how to get back to the bridge. He gave us a strange look.

"You're standing on it."

It was another embarrassing moment, with more hysterical laughter. Somehow, we had gotten turned around again. You couldn't see the water from the bridge. Because it looked so much like a street, we didn't realize where we were.

That night, when we met up with the others, Ethel and Lucy had everyone in stitches as we told them about all our mishaps. We also told them about our expensive glasses of wine. Every time we told them about an interesting place we had discovered, such as the Fountain of Neptune, they would ask, "Where did you find that? We never saw it." and we would answer, "We have no idea. We were lost the whole time."

Most of the other B & B people were retired teachers who were very organized. They had their maps and travel guides and their museum reservations all made, while Sue and I preferred to travel by the seats of our pants. We would just start off and see where we ended up.

The next morning was our "D-day." We were now becoming familiar with the streets and didn't have any trouble finding our way to the Duomo, the Cathedral of Saint Mary of the Flower. The building of the cathedral began in 1296 and it wasn't completed until 1436. It is the fourth largest church in the world. I googled its "steps" and the entry said that climbing the steps is one of the most challenging activities you can do in Florence. Google was right; that climb wasn't for the faint of heart. I already knew that! Our Jason certainly wasn't faint of heart, that's for sure.

As soon as we entered the Duomo, we could feel its spirituality. It was a sacred place and we were in awe of its beauty. It was vast, with shiny marble floors that covered the large, open area, inside. Above us, detailed fresco artwork adorned the massive ceiling. It was overwhelming in its beauty and magnificence. We were drawn to the candle stands where visitors can light candles for their loved ones. Lighting a candle for Mark and Jason was a powerful moment for me, a very important part of my journey.

After taking a few moments to reflect, Sue and I began our long climb up the narrow, ancient stone stairway that wound between the two outer walls. Every once in a while, we would have to press against the wall on one side, or the other, to let people pass. A few times, we had to crouch down to go through the tunnel where the ceiling was sloped and low. Along the way, we found occasional openings where it was possible to peer down into the chapel below. More significantly, it was possible to look at the ceiling frescos which seemed closer, with each flight we climbed. When we reached the first balcony, we felt that we could almost reach out and touch the paintings.

We were getting weary, but the awe of our surroundings gave us the energy to keep going. The view from the second balcony was even more stunning – we almost seemed to be part of the fresco painting of *The Last Judgment*. The fine details, and depth of the colours, made it appear three-dimensional.

We finally made it to the top. I went out onto the balcony rooftop to take in the view over Florence. It was breathless, in more ways than one, after climbing 463 stairs!

Unfortunately, Sue was terrified of heights. She said that if she went near the edge, she would feel like jumping off. The sensation of being so high up seemed to take over her body, exerting a tremendous pull on her. She had braved this climb for my sake. When we got to the top, Sue sat against the wall, and waited for me until I walked all the way around the dome, so I could take in all the views. I felt free, uplifted. I wondered how Jay would feel about me being there. I'm sure that he would have understood the joy it gave me.

As we wound our way down the steps, our alter egos, Ethel and Lucy, got turned around again. We started giggling and were shushed by a guard. Somehow, we had managed to exit through the entrance. The guards, at the entrance, looked confused but let us pass. Only we could do something like that.

We felt both moved and elated, when we came out into the Duomo courtyard. We found a nice little cafe on a side street and decided to have a gin and tonic to celebrate. This time we stood at the bar. The young bartender couldn't help but notice how sentimental we were being. As we sipped our gin, we reminisced about raising our sons, about losing my boys, about life in general. There were tears in our eyes as we talked. The young man brought us a sandwich to split and enough olives and cheese to feed a small group.

"Enjoy," he said. "It's on the house."

We thanked him for his generosity, but we noticed his superior was upset with him. We saw him shrug as he explained the situation. It's true, Italian men can be very passionate and caring. When we got our bill, we discovered that we had only been charged five Euros for our full-course lunch as well as two very large gin and tonics. It was a great improvement over the fifteen Euros we had paid the day before. Maybe we were catching on to this Italian thing!

And in the sweetness of friendship, let there be laughter,
and sharing of pleasures. For in the dew of little things
the heart finds its morning and is refreshed.

PAULO COELHO, THE PILGRIMAGE

Sue sent me the above quote, in a birthday card.

Our visit to Italy was nearly over, and we were becoming seasoned travelers. I bought a three-quarter-length, leather swing coat at the market; that was another true Italian experience.

Sue and I went looking for the train station, as we planned to take a train to Pisa a couple of days later. I also wanted to find the location of the Hotel Paris, where I was planning to stay one night, by myself, before flying out. According to the Internet, the hotel was Florence's best-kept secret. The reviewers must have been right because we couldn't find it. Ethel and Lucy must have looked confused because an

American woman approached us, to see if we needed help. She told us that she had been living in Florence, with her husband, for the last five years. We asked if she knew the location of the hotel. We showed her the address, but she couldn't find it, either.

She invited us to her apartment to look it up on the Internet. We followed her to a luxury apartment building with marble floors and at least fourteen-foot ceilings. She introduced us to her husband and we tracked down the location of the hotel. Our impromptu hostess insisted on coming back with us, to make sure we found it.

We weren't disappointed. The front-desk clerk was very proud of the Hotel Paris, and gave us a tour. The small hotel had been an old mansion and was decorated in the older Italian style with amazing antique furniture and beautiful architecture details. An elevator, the size of a closet, added to the quaintness. Sue was disappointed that she wouldn't be staying there with me.

The rest of the trip went just as well. Our group moved to Villa Steffi, which was nestled amongst rolling hills located near the small town of Cortona. *Under the Tuscan Sun* was filmed in Cortona and apparently the author of the book still lived in a villa near us. Our hostess Steffi and her family welcomed us with a delicious, authentic pasta dish, and plenty of their homemade wine. We took day trips from our villa to villages like Montepulciano and Siena. It was such a treat to drive to the towns on single-lane, winding roads surrounded by a landscape of sand-coloured stucco villas on hillsides covered in vineyards, long rows of tall cypress trees and splashes of yellow sunflowers. The towns were all quite similar, surrounded by stone-walled fortresses, with courtyards, a Roman Catholic Church, shuttered windows and winding cobblestone streets with tiny stone staircases leading to local dwellings. There was usually a vantage point where you could take in the wonderful views that are Tuscany's trademark. At the end of the day, we would either stop at a wonderful village *ristorante* and fill up on delicious pasta dishes and fine Chianti wines, or take turns cooking at the villa. One day, Sue and I took a three-mile walk to a nearby village for lunch. It was worth the effort because walking helped us appreciate the landscape even more. I fell in love with Italy and would go back in a heartbeat.

Sue and I said our goodbyes to the rest of the group and took the train to Pisa. We went to see the Leaning Tower and took a few pictures before we had our last dinner together. Sue was taking a plane home while I was returning to Florence the next day. Hotel Paris was within walking distance of the train station and was easy to find this time. I would recommend it to anyone.

I spent my last day in Florence alone, visiting the magnificent Boboli Gardens that are situated behind the Pitti Palace. I walked the garden paths, among the many sculptures that were scattered throughout the property. It was a peaceful place to reflect and relax on my last day in Italy. When I am travelling alone in a distant land, I often feel that my boys are looking out for me and guiding me. On the last night, I enjoyed a quiet meal in a charming little pasta *ristorante* across from the hotel, where I chatted with two women who were travelling separately. The owner was a chubby, elderly gentleman with tiny spectacles perched on his stubby little nose. He added to the atmosphere with the twinkle in his eye as he made me feel welcome. I felt totally at peace.

The next day, I flew to London where I caught a train to Edinburgh, Scotland. My sister Cathy and her family were spending a week there, so I decided to join then. After all, I was almost in the neighbourhood!

Scotland was very different from Italy. The Italian accordions were replaced by the echoing sound of pipes playing in the distance. The narrow, cobbled, streets of Italy were replaced by busy intersections and newer buildings, but they still seemed ancient by Canadian standards. I was surrounded by evidence of Scotland's proud history. I immediately fell in love with Scotland and the Scottish people.

Edinburgh had its famous castle and monuments, parks and red double-decker buses. The tiny bistros were replaced by Scottish pubs. The Balmoral Hotel, where I stayed, had an indoor pool where I could swim while enjoying a perfect view of Edinburgh Castle which is perched on the hill above the city. The concierge was extremely helpful, while the dining room staff made me feel very special. They called me by name as they served their delicious Scottish dishes. I acquired a taste for haggis, which was served in the breakfast buffet.

The next day, I moved to another hotel to rendezvous with Cathy and her family. I discovered that my girlfriend, Pam, who lived in Liverpool, had decided to drive up to join me for a couple of days. We had met in Canada when we were teenagers, and had kept in touch ever since. We all explored Edinburgh together and then said our goodbyes to Pam, before taking the train to the Highland district in northern Scotland. Cathy had a time-share rented in a little village called Kenmore, situated where Loch Tay drains into the Tay River. We felt as though we were in a time warp. Things hadn't changed in the village for centuries. There was a very old inn on the river bank surrounded by white cottages with black trim, and white picket fences. Our time-share was within walking distance across a tiny stone bridge. The next day, we took a walk along the river trail and found the abandoned Taymouth Castle at the end of the path. We couldn't believe it. There was a fence around it but we could explore all the grounds, which included old stone buildings, defence towers and gates. We felt like children who had discovered a hidden secret place.

We drove to Saint Andrews Golf Club, which was a dream for Cathy's husband. On the way back, we got lost, which bothered everyone else, but seemed normal for me. That night, we enjoyed supper in the old Kenmore Inn whose owners claim is the oldest in Scotland (although someone later told us that a lot of inns say the same thing).

After dinner, everyone left me sitting at the table, as I needed an emotional pause, because *Amazing Grace* was playing over the sound system, and I wanted a moment to let it soak in. The two handsome waiters came over to see if I was alright. I explained that the song had a special meaning to me. I asked where they were from because they both had accents. One was from Florence, and the other was from Spain. Those were both places that Jason and Sarah had visited. Nice!

A few days later, Cathy's family took the train back to London and I went back to Edinburgh where I planned to spend one last night before flying home. I felt like royalty as the old black cab took me past the gatehouse and up the long driveway through picturesque grounds to the Dalmahoy Marriott Hotel and Golf Club. It was built in 1725 and, apparently, Mary Queen of Scots had once stayed there. Now it was my turn. Once I got settled, I enjoyed a dip in the indoor pool and then decided to take a stroll around the property. The grounds were lovely. I was drawn back down the driveway towards the gatehouse. As I crossed over an old stone bridge, I watched the stream meander by as horses grazed on the hillside. At the end of the road, I was drawn to an ancient church, nestled amongst a grove of trees. Intrigued, I reverently entered the grounds, stopping to read a plaque. It stated that the church was built by a former estate owner as a gift for his wife. Apparently, his wife had died shortly after the church was completed.

I couldn't help feeling the love that surrounded this very special place. There was a single stained-glass window with the image of a mother and child; its significance was not lost on me. On a stone bench, set amongst some trees, I rested to soak in the solitude. I reflected on my journey and thought about my boys and my Dad, who had recently passed away. He had left me just enough money to make this trip possible.

As I sat there, I noticed an unkempt garden at the far side of the grounds. When I walked over to it, I saw a small plaque with the words "A dearly beloved family man now in God's hands." Underneath the marker was a tiny stone with the word "Papa".

As I stood there, feeling very moved, I heard some leaves rustling behind the garden. When I glanced in the direction of the movement, I saw two tiny rabbits playing together amongst the undergrowth. I immediately thought of Mark, Jason and Papa who were now at peace and free to enjoy this special place with me. What a perfect ending to my pilgrimage.

A heart at peace, gives life to the body

PROVERBS 14:30

FINDING JOY

A Stroke Becomes a
Blessing in Disguise

Life was taking its toll on Bill and me. It had been almost four years since we had lost Jason and a couple of years since we had lost my Dad. One Friday, I was feeling a bit light-headed and unwell at work. On the way to the washroom, I staggered a bit, then was sick to my stomach. Nurse Kim immediately picked up on it and the next thing I knew, I was sitting in my family doctor's office being checked out. I knew that they were wondering if I might be having a stroke.

I was very dizzy. Every time I moved, I felt sick to my stomach. I was suffering from vertigo, so they phoned Bill to come and get me. He came with two neighbours, one of whom drove us home, while the other drove my car back. I had strict orders to spend the weekend resting. I didn't argue. The way I was feeling, I couldn't do anything else.

We were a very tight-knit community and later that afternoon, another couple of neighbours came to see if I was alright. One mentioned that Bill looked very tired and pale and seemed to be a bit off. That night, when Bill said good night, he staggered a bit and laughed about it. I never thought anything of it because Bill has been known to stagger a bit on occasion.

In the middle of the night, I woke up because Bill's arm around me seemed very heavy. When I asked him to roll over, he began to fumble and said he couldn't. I got up, turned on the light and immediately realized that he was having a stroke. His face had drooped and he couldn't move one side. I ran to call 911. By the time I got back to the room, Bill was lying on the floor and couldn't get up. I looked in his drawer for a shirt to put on him, but every one of them said something like "Beer is not just for breakfast" or "Beer is man's best friend," or the one I hated the most that said, "I'm not an alcoholic, I'm a drunk. Alcoholics go to meetings." I finally found something more suitable. It gave us something to laugh about in the middle of the scary situation we were facing. Bill was probably in shock, but he was still in good spirits. The ambulance arrived and the medics put him on a special chair to get him down our steep stairs. They roared off while I followed in the car. Thank goodness my adrenalin had kicked in. I was feeling well enough to drive.

It turned out that Bill's blood pressure was so high that he blew a blood vessel in his brain. The bleed caused the stroke. The first step was to get his blood pressure down. The hospital staff took him to intensive care and all we could do was wait, and see. There was a chance Bill might not make it, or that he might end up in a wheelchair for the rest of his life.

About forty-eight hours later, Bill started to go through withdrawal. Dr. Kent and I once more teamed up to help a member of my family. It was a nightmare trying to hold Bill down, while the nurse gave him medication. I knew the nurse and at one point, I tried to make a joke, saying, "Welcome to the skeleton in my closet." We all survived that night. I wish now that we had taken a video – I think that if Bill saw that video, he would never want to drink again.

Bill spent a month in our local hospital and was lucky to have a lot of friends who came to visit him. During the first two weeks, he couldn't even sit up on his own. Dr. Kent said he wouldn't be eligible for a rehab hospital unless he could sit up by himself and handle a wheelchair. He seemed to be out of danger at the moment, so Dr. Kent had a heart-to-heart talk with him. He explained that the rest was up to him, whether he improved, or didn't. Bill started physiotherapy and was finally accepted to Penetang Rehabilitation. He remembers very little about his one-month stay in hospital. He says that he feels as if he lost a section of his life. I guess the mind has a way of protecting us.

I began noticing a change in Bill's personality. He always had a smile on his face and had lost his gloom and doom. He felt lucky to be alive and was finally able to stop sweating the small stuff. In the past, he would often take the easy way out; if things seemed difficult, he would have just given up. Now he was faced with the biggest challenge of his life, and he held firm. When they said it would be up to him, whether he walked again or not, he said, "Just watch me."

Bill loved the nurses at Penetang, and every morning, he was the first in line for therapy. When I went to see him, he was in good spirits and was excited about every little triumph. He saw that there were patients with missing limbs and realized that he was much better off. Bill spent another two months in Penetang. Every week, when I went to see him, I could see an improvement. He would always be waiting for me, in his wheelchair, at the entrance, with a big grin. I brought him home for a couple of days over Christmas and we made a date for New Year's Eve. We welcomed 2012 in a nice Penetang retirement home that had a view of the lake.

I was sad when I had no shoes until I met a man with no feet.

PROVERB

Bill went into Penetang in a wheelchair, and came home able to walk without a cane. Finally luck was with us.

Even today, Bill makes a visit at Christmas and usually in the spring, to see his girls at Penetang. He takes them treats of chocolates and other goodies, to show his gratitude.

Having a stroke can sometimes change a person's personality. They can either get grumpy and miserable, or become thankful and happy. I remember an old patient at the office who had been miserable his whole life. He was also very demanding of his wife and the office staff.

When he had a stroke, he changed. His daughter brought him into the office a few times and we talked about it. She said she felt cheated out of her childhood and wondered why it took a stroke to find the loving father she had craved her whole life. She was still angry with him, but glad that they still had an opportunity to make up for some of the bad times.

I told Bill we would have to sell the house on Lake of Bays. It was too much for us to handle financially. Besides, the long drive to work every day was taking its toll on me. It was getting too hard physically to look after the grounds and clean such a big house. If we were in town, I could come home for lunch instead of leaving him alone all day. Bill agreed, but he wasn't happy about it.

When the house went on the market, we realized that we had a problem – our dock and waterfront weren't transferable to the new owners. I spent the next few months involved in very stressful negotiations with council, in hopes of finding a remedy to the situation. After many letters, and attending township meetings, we acquired a lease that could be transferred to the new owners. The old B & B was sold to a family with lots of grandchildren who were going to use it as a cottage. I was so happy that this wonderful old homestead would be alive again with young people enjoying my beloved Lake of Bays.

I knew it was time for a change; Bill, not so much. The whole first year after we moved, he just sat in his La-Z-Boy watching television. Finally, he declared that we had bought a good house and that living in town wasn't so bad after all.

Thank goodness.

> **Happiness** *is a state of mind. Very little is needed to make a happy life. It is all within yourself in your way of thinking.*
>
> **MARCUS AURELUIS**

Bill has never held me back when I wanted to travel, even though he had no interest in joining me. He accepted that I loved to try new things, to go out with lots of different friends, as long as I didn't make him come along or join in. He also realizes how important this book is to me. I appreciate him for that.

Had we been soul mates, I never would have met so many interesting people who have played an important part in shaping my life. I never would have learned to be as independent as I am, and to do things on my own. My parents never understood this. They thought that I should be a better wife and stay home with my husband. They thought it would cause trouble in my marriage. They didn't realize that I was trying to survive the marriage.

When the boys were young, all I ever wanted was to be at home with them, to be together as a family. I baked, had a big vegetable garden and made preserves. They were my life and I'm so glad that I had that time with them. But as they grew, I had to grow as well. I never wanted to risk becoming stagnant and broken. The childrearing years represented another rocky time in our marriage. I knew the only way to please my parents, and Bill, and survive, was to make myself stronger. I needed to be more independent, to become a more rounded person. Love and our marriage have always seemed like an endurance test for me. It has made me stronger but not without playing havoc with my emotional life. I still have trouble crying. My friends tell me that I have always tried to please everyone except myself. They were right. But maybe that was my choice and my role in life.

Eventually, Bill had not only accepted living in town, but also thought that he might want to start travelling. He even suggested that we visit Peter and Heather, our friends who wintered in Cyprus. They had been asking us to visit for years.

Cyprus! This, from the same man who thought going to Toronto was too big a deal; the man who would never get on a plane because he thought it might crash. Bill had always seen the big, old, world out there as a place that was waiting to get him. The stroke must have shorted out that part of his brain.

Whatever happened, I certainly wasn't going to complain. I got on the computer and told him that if we were going to Cyprus, we might as well stop off in Greece. There was a small cruise of the Greek Islands and Turkey that would fit into our itinerary quite nicely. He bucked a bit at the cruise idea because he can't swim and hated all boats. I assured him that it was only for three nights, and that the Mediterranean was a good place to try out cruising. He agreed and we ended up having a great holiday. Bill loved the cruise. He was hooked.

Attitude: *The difference between an adventure and an ordeal.*

UNKNOWN

It's now 2014; I have retired after twenty-five years at the doctor's office and Bill and I have just celebrated our forty-fifth wedding anniversary. We went to Alaska to celebrate. It is now the autumn of my life. With the extra money from selling the house, along with the money Dad and Mom left us, we have enough to live on, with a little extra to travel. I am thankful that I have this opportunity to find some peace and joy and to make the best of the time we have left. It's our turn.

Bill and I are becoming travelers. Travelling opens our hearts and minds to new places, new adventures, new foods and tastes, to new people and the wonders of the world. It gets us away from the everyday humdrum of normal life. It also makes us aware of how lucky we are to live in Canada. We appreciate home a little more.

Five years ago, Tee gave birth to a little boy, named Emmett. We are blessed because he calls us Nana and Papa. Emmett, Tee and I just got back from celebrating Emmett's fifth birthday at Disney World in Florida. Just like Mark, he enjoyed the rides.

It brings me joy when Emmett and I snuggle up for a story. I tell him that I love him, from the tip of his head to the bottom of his toes and everything in between. When I tickle him, in between, it brings us both joy. This summer, after going to Santa's Village, I found him a used two-wheeler bike and helmet, at the Sally Ann store. By the time his Mom came to pick him up that night, he had learned to ride off by himself. The three of us were bouncing up and down with joy.

Life is pretty good at the moment and I am smiling at lot these days. I just heard on CBC that smiling is good for us. Writing this book has been draining and painful at times, but it has also worked wonders for my spiritual self, as well as my mental health. Now that I'm retired, I enjoy concentrating on my physical health and wellbeing. I have joined the Sportsplex, with its many classes and the walking track. It's a great opportunity to meet a lot of nice people who are working towards the same goals. After all, travelling and living life to the fullest isn't for sissies.

Don't Quit

When things go wrong as they sometimes will,
When the road you're trudging seems all uphill,
When the funds are low and the debts are high,
And you want to smile, but you have to sigh,
When care is pressing you down a bit
Rest if you must, but don't quit.
Success is failure turned inside out.
The silver tint of the clouds of doubt
And you never can tell how close you are,
It may be near when it seems afar
So stick to the fight, when you are hardest hit
It's when things go wrong that you mustn't quit.

AUTHOR UNKNOWN

I found this on a small wallet card in 1994. It helped me then and maybe it will help someone else. At the time I found this card, I thought my life was hard. This was even before I lost the boys. At the time, I had no idea what life had in store for me.

Let's think of a different scenario. If I hadn't held onto my lifeline of my memories, of my time with the boys and all my responsibilities, I would have drowned in my sorrows. If I had decided to go through that door instead of staying in my white hallway, I would have fallen into the abyss and been lost. This book would have been called, *Finding Pain: A Mother's Losses and How They Ruined Her Life.*

My friends would be gone. They would be tired of attending pity parties. I would probably have lost my job; we might have lost our home. Bill and I would probably still be together, but we would have existed as two bitter, angry individuals, who hated each other and everything around us. The memory of our sons would have been tarnished and forgotten.

"Losing their sons destroyed them," people would say.

What would that have done to our sons' spirits, if they looked down and witnessed what their dying had done to us? It makes me sad just writing this.

Enough! I'm getting back into my box of joy – a much better place to be, with my boys cheering me on.

My Past Lives

We lost Mom in March 2013. Now that we've both lost our parents, as well as our two sons, Bill and I have decided to make a new tradition of skipping Christmas. I love taking part in the buildup and hype of the seasonal parties, food, shopping, colourful lights, and the feeling of closeness to family and friends. However, we both prefer to escape Christmas Day because it is just a reminder of what we no longer have.

New Orleans was always on my bucket list because of its interesting history, sense of mystery and exciting musical atmosphere. I also knew that New Orleans was very spiritual. When I discovered that it was a cruise ship port, it was a no-brainer to go there for Christmas.

Bill and I liked New Orleans – the variety of Cajun and French cuisine, culture, blues and jazz and its surroundings, make it an exhila-rating place to visit. I couldn't get over how happy the people seemed, despite their adversity, tragedy and the hard times brought on by Hurricane Katrina. We booked into a charming historic hotel, within walking distance of the French Quarter. The next day, we went on a bus tour to get our bearings in the city. Included on the tour was a walk through a raised cemetery (because of the high water table, and the constant threats of flooding, the cemeteries in New Orleans consist of raised cement crypts). Apparently, when they opened some of the vaults, they discovered that some poor individuals had been buried alive while in comas! To mitigate this problem, they began tying a string on the toe of each corpse, with a bell on the end of the toe. The bell hung outside the vault. A watchman was hired for the "graveyard shift" to listen for "dead ringers." The vaults got so humid due to the New Orleans climate that the bodies decayed very quickly. As subsequent bodies were put into the same vaults, grave workers would push the previous body parts through slots, in the back of the vaults, so they would fall into the bottom section with the other poor souls. Their tool of choice was a ten-foot pole. That's where the saying, "I wouldn't touch him with a ten-foot pole," came from. Just a little New Orleans trivia.

We ventured out, in the evening, to find an interesting place for dinner. We came across a side street, closed to traffic, where several gypsy-like people sat, at small tables. They wore shawls and colourful clothing, had candles glowing, and tarot cards, ready to do readings for the curious passers-by. Of course, I couldn't resist paying twenty dollars to hear my future. It couldn't have been very exciting because I can't even remember what the reader told me.

When I worked at the doctor's office, one of my co-workers had mentioned that her sister went to a psychic where she had her past lives read. The thought of discovering past lives intrigued me – I often thought that I must have been evil in a past life. Was I a murderer? Or something worse? Was losing the boys a punishment for something I had done?

Now that I was in New Orleans, it was going to be my mission to find out. At the hotel, I brought up the subject with the young woman behind the desk.

"You might think I'm crazy," I began, "But I would like to have my past lives read and I wonder if you know of anyone who does it."

She answered that this was New Orleans – of course she didn't think I was crazy.

"We take these matters very seriously," she said. "The psychics are even monitored by the city."

She told me she had her own past lives read and advised me not to go to anyone on the street. In her opinion, there was only one person who was really reliable. She would see if she could track her down for me; she made a couple of calls, and told me where the lady was going to be the following day.

The next day, I set off on my mission. Bill and I headed out to the address I had been given; we found a bar close by where Bill could wait for me. The meeting place was pretty much what I expected: a long, narrow, dingy little shop. Behind the shopkeeper, at a cluttered counter, hung an array of masks, necklaces, dolls and various types of incense. An obligatory bead curtain hung from a doorway leading into another room in the back. I told the shopkeeper why I was there and when I mentioned past lives, she was hesitant. She said that the reader didn't do those kinds of readings anymore because it was too hard on her. She said that she would ask and went through the beaded entrance to speak to the reader. Thank goodness, the psychic agreed to do a reading, just for me.

I nervously made my way into a back room which was the size of a large walk-in closet. Sitting behind a small card table, on an old wooden chair, was an elderly woman with long grey hair and wrinkled, dark skin. I couldn't help thinking that she resembled Della Reese from *Touched by an Angel*. I could tell she wasn't well – I'd been told that she had health problems – because she looked tired and drawn and there was a walker sitting in the corner. Speaking in an accent, she invited me to have a seat. We chatted a bit, getting to know each other a little, before we began. She told me that she had moved to New Orleans from South Africa.

Impatient to begin, I blurted out that I had lost my two boys, and wondered if I had ticked off somebody in another life, and that's why these bad things had happened to me. She took a breath and instructed me to just relax, to sit quietly for five minutes with my eyes shut. Then she gave me permission to open them.

"Very interesting," she said. "I don't see anything you did in your past lives to upset anyone; quite the opposite. As a matter of fact, your boys chose you."

According to the psychic, I lived my first life in England, during the time of Henry VIII. I had been a Catholic, who was very upset with

Henry VIII for separating the church. But I got over it and got on with my life. I was married and looked after the poor and the sick with a friend, who came from a distance to help me prepare soup and special herbs for them. Because it was too great a distance for her to travel, she taught me to make the soups and to gather the herbs. That seemed to be my mission in that life.

My next life took place in the 1800s. I was a nun, and lived in a convent, located a wagon ride away from Montreal, Quebec. My mission was to look after and teach orphan boys. Apparently, I was happy looking after the boys and lived a very fulfilled life. (When I got home, I looked up convents near Montreal and learned on Google. that there were several in the area. The nuns there often taught school, and looked after orphans.)

My third life wasn't a life at all. I was a spirit hovering over the trenches during World War II. My job was to bring fallen soldiers up into the light. The psychic said that she could visualize German and English spirits going up together.

The life I have now is my fourth one. Apparently, I was chosen to give my boys love; she felt that I had accomplished my mission. She knew, without me telling her, that Mark had committed suicide. She also said that one of my boys had had a past life in a dysfunctional home; his mother drank and beat him. I just knew that it had to be Jason. Until he was about five, I noticed he acted strange at times. His behavior resembled a child that had been beaten. One time, while my Grandfather was visiting, we were sitting at the table and my Grandfather raised his voice to explain something. Jay immediately got up and ran off. When I went to look for him, I found him in our garage, curled up in the fetal position, on the floor of the back seat of the car. I asked him what the matter was. He said he didn't know. A couple of other times, he ran and hid for no apparent reason. He didn't know why. He very seldom cried, but he could take a lot of pain when he got hurt. He very seldom complained when he was sick. The sound of children crying also bothered him. The psychic added that, when Jason died, she felt he went back to help his dysfunctional mother. I didn't completely understand that part.

I was really glad to have had my past lives read. It gave me some peace of mind. I don't know whether we really do have past lives, but there are so many things that we don't understand. As far as I'm concerned, anything is possible. I thought it was funny that I was a strict Catholic in two other lives and now I'm Protestant and not really very religious at all. My religion is love, kindness and forgiveness; my credo is "Do unto others as you would have them do unto you."

A friend recently suggested that religion was like a mountain, with the top representing the ultimate goal. People practicing different religions have the same goal – to reach the top of the mountain. We just have different paths to get there. I like that metaphor.

I do see some similarities between this life and my past lives. I worked in a doctor's office and cared for people who were ill. I also loved to take care of my boys and I still keep an eye on the boys who were friends of my sons.

This past Christmas, we escaped to Texas. While I was exploring a side street in Galveston, I was happy to discover a tiny used book store where I could find a cheap book to take on the next day's cruise. As I wandered down an aisle, looking for something light to read, like a romance novel, I saw instead the book *Past Lives, Future Healing* by Sylvia Browne. It seemed to almost fall into my hand. This book was a very interesting read. Sylvia Browne is well respected in the medical field and often sees patients who can't be cured by traditional methods. Hypothetically, she might have seen someone who developed lung and breathing problems at around age thirty, a condition that couldn't be explained by CAT scans and breathing tests. While under hypnosis and past-life regression, the patient would learn that he had died of smoke inhalation, around the same age, in a past life. When he realizes it was just his memory cells from a past life, he is able to let those memories go. That would be the cure.

I thought back to my conversation with the thirty-something hotel clerk in New Orleans. She told me that she had terrible hip pain that

couldn't be explained. When she had her past lives read, she discovered
that she had been tortured in a past life and her hip had been crushed.
Once she was aware of it, the hip pain vanished. Her case was similar to
cases in Sylvia Browne's book.

I was intrigued by Browne's idea of our spirits returning, over and
over again. I must admit, it makes a lot of sense to me. I loved her
theory that when we die, our spirit goes to the white light of the Holy
Spirit, where it is cleansed. Once the spirit is cleansed, it travels into
another womb to begin its next life. Apparently, we have a choice about
the kind of life we enter. Sometimes we carry cell memory with us
to the next life, which would explain Jason's fear of being beaten, and
Mark wanting to be a clown.

According to Browne, evil spirits don't go to the white light to be
cleansed – they have chosen to devote their energy to destroying anything light and good. They go through a hollow, bottomless, Godless
void called the Left Door on the dark side and then horseshoe back
to continue their destructive ways, in their next lives. Those possessed
with evil wouldn't want their past lives read because they are suspi-
cious. In fact, the past lives of evil spirits can't be read because they
have walls up to guard them.

This is just my interpretation of her book. You would have to read
it yourself to get a better idea. But wouldn't it be interesting if we could
shed a little light on those dark souls, so they could open themselves up
to the light of love and caring? The world would certainly be a kinder,
less selfish place. I would be happy to bring even one spirit to the light.

I Finally Get It

Writing this book has been a device for my own self-discovery and self-questioning. I believe that thinking more fully about the lessons I have learned, as well as accepting and understanding the events that have occurred in my life, is another important part of my journey. Will I ever have all the answers? I doubt it. But isn't that part of the wonderful mystery of life?

It has brought me joy to finally finish something that I started. I hope that I will come out the other side as a more compassionate, more complete and better person. When I have been thrown into a bad situation, I have always tried to roll with the punches. Like a chameleon, I have tried to adapt to my new situation. Sometimes, that can be a good thing; other times, not so much.

One of the most important lessons I have learned is to accept what I can't change and accept my life as it is. My Mom always had the wonderful ability to accept things that were thrown her way. She just kept navigating her way through life, with a steady hand on the helm, keeping herself on an even keel. Maybe she had more faith than I do. When her lymphoma was progressing and she was losing strength, I asked if she ever thought about dying.

"No," she answered, "I haven't really thought about it."

Even on her last day, she insisted on getting dressed and carrying on as usual. Maybe she was trying to protect me, or maybe she was in denial. I just know that I truly admire her.

Surviving the hardships of life can be a struggle for all of us. I guess we all have different coping mechanisms that make the difference between whether we succeed or fail, whether we are content or frustrated, whether we are always searching for a beacon to guide us to the euphoria that we think we deserve. Some people are the type who feel that they are already home, securely moored in a familiar safe harbour. I'm a Gemini, the sign of the twins, and feel that both parts make up my personality – the part that is content, and the part that always seems to be searching. That can be complicated.

Acceptance has also helped my relationship with Bill. Now that we have learned to accept each other the way we are, without huge expectations, things run much more smoothly. We are actually able to laugh about our flaws, without getting defensive or angry. We are comfortable with who we are. We have an "it is what it is" philosophy.

Having so many different kinds of friends has also helped me to question myself, and to be open to new ideas. I once told my friend, Mary, that my most important lesson was acceptance.

"Where do you draw the line on how much acceptance is too much and when to say no more?" she asked.

Good question. She was right. Maybe it's more about "accepting the things that we can't change and changing the things we can."

If someone is in an abusive relationship, then acceptance would be out of the question. I guess it is an individual decision and choice.

Writing this book has allowed me to open up a new dialogue with myself and discuss my ideas with other people, so that I can discover different avenues of thinking. It has also introduced me to several writers' groups that have taught me that there is a whole other world out there which includes fiction, imagination, humour, expression, vocabulary, and description. It has given me a desire to expand my capacity to learn new words and their meanings. And it has given me a desire to push myself, to be a better storyteller. We are never too old to improve, to open ourselves to new ideas. As long as we are alive, we must never stop thinking and learning.

Finally, I always try to appreciate that my glass is half-full, rather than half-empty. That way, I can savour and rejoice in what I have, instead of fretting over what I have lost or what I am missing. In other words, I try to concentrate on the positives in my life, rather than the negatives. It isn't easy, and I have to constantly keep reminding myself to be thankful. We in North America are so lucky to be living where we live. In some countries, people's glasses are almost empty, and they likely have barely a few drops of hope left to keep them going.

I hope that my journey has been of some assistance in your life, or has, at least, given you something to think about. I am constantly asked how I survived. Everyone seems to be looking for a secret, magic pill, a quick fix, or an easy explanation. As you can see, there isn't one. It is a constant battle to keep going, but I will always keep forging on. I have a lot of people counting on me, including myself and my boys, and I will never let them down. I am ready to face whatever life has in store for me. Looking back, I realize that there has been a constant thread woven through all the parts of my journey: the power of love. My love for the boys, which gave me purpose, my love for family and friends, my love for my patients and my co-workers at the clinic, my love of nature and Mother Earth, my love of life and for discovering new ideas and adventures.

I finally get it. The power of love is the secret to finding joy.

I would like to conclude this with one of Jason's favourite sayings and one of mine: "Let's keep rocking in the free world."

And this one.

"Count our blessings, not our woes, and enjoy the power of love."

Joy

For me, the meaning of joy is feeling some peace, or contentment – a tiny moment that will put a smile on my face or, more importantly, a smile in my heart. It is just a hint of a euphoric, heavenly, experience that gives me a sense of deep pleasure. Of course, there isn't a day that I don't struggle with life and I don't expect to feel joy every day, but I am thankful that I can feel joy at all. There were times in my life when I thought that joy was gone forever.

Everyone has their own individual definition of joy, but I would like to share with you a few things that have brought me joy, in the last couple of weeks.

My Own List of Joys

It brings me joy when I smile from my heart and someone smiles back.

It brings me joy when I hold a newborn child.

It brings me joy when I see a young father holding his daughter, or son, with the look of love, wonder, and adoration.

It brings me joy when a man is comfortable enough with his own masculinity to carry his wife's cute, and feminine, beach bag over his shoulder, while holding a folded-up stroller in one hand and towels in the other. He isn't giving it a thought; he's just looking forward to the day's adventure.

It brings me joy to wake up to a sunny day, or to a rainy day if the grass needs watering and I want an excuse to sleep in.

It brings me joy to go to an exercise class, and watch an eighty-year-old keep up with the young ones.

It brings me joy when I think of my sons and cherish a memory.

It brings me joy when Tee's son calls me Nana, while we enjoy snuggling, and planning our next adventure.

It brings me joy when I have a night with my sisters.

It brings me joy when I take a warm, soothing, shower and as the water caresses, refreshes and cleanses my body, I feel grateful for such a luxury that we all take for granted.

It brings me joy when ....

The point is, thankfully, that I could fill a book with the things that bring me moments of joy. With the state of our world, these days, I think we all need a little joy. Maybe the next time you feel joy, you should write it down, or at least store it in a memory.

Wishing you a little joy,

Jude

(Like Jason, I use several names. Judith is my given name, but everyone has always called me Judy. My closest friends most often call me "Jude.")

MY MEMORY GARDEN

Introduction

Now that you have read about my journey, I would like to take you on a stroll through the garden that exists in my memory. Gardening has helped me through a very difficult time in my life. It gave me time to think, to reflect on, and appreciate, the beauty of the world. Please come with me, and let me share the lessons I learned through this amazing experience.

Did you know that, when people see a certain flower, it sparks a memory of someone they know or have known? When friends stroll through my garden, for example, they may say, "Oh, you have gladiolas! Those were my mother's favourite flowers!"

This is usually followed by a slight hesitation and a smile, as they experience a memory. Everyone, in Canada, of a certain age remembers Pierre Trudeau wearing a single rose in his lapel; it became his signature. When I think of Trudeau, I always see the rose. In the same way, the flowers I have chosen for my Memory Garden represent a few people who have awakened some memory, or taught me some kind of lesson. As you read these short stories, you will find that we inherit traits from our roots that follow us through our entire lives. Having this root system has aided in my ability to understand who we are. How we deal with life creates an environment that also has a lasting effect on those around us.

There is a book written about the first three people a man meets in heaven. When he first arrives in heaven, the man is surprised to see that the first people he meets are not his loved ones. Instead, they are virtual strangers, people he has touched without even realizing it. I think of Barb when I think of this story about a "chance meeting".

Lavender

Lavender

Barb had a confident kind of glow about her, punctuated with sassy, spiked grey hair, just the right amount of makeup, with mascara that had smeared a little beneath her sparkling, dark eyes. Her tasteful jewelry complemented the lovely grey shawl that she wrapped grace-fully around her shoulders.

We exchanged smiles as I plunked down beside her on the airport shuttle bus.

Immediately, I felt comfortable in her presence. As we struck up an easy conversation, she told me that she had had a happy marriage and successful children, whom she adored. Her husband had died a few years before and she was now quite content with her life, and her memories. Friends would try to set her up, but she insisted that she had been lucky once and didn't want to take another chance. Who would have guessed that she would meet a man in Florida, with whom she felt very comfortable. They enjoyed the same things and shared similar friends. Now she was on her way to spend the winter with him. One of her old Aunts had once told her never to die wondering, so she figured he was worth a chance.

While we were talking, we also discovered that she had gone to school in Niagara Falls, with a dear cottage neighbour and friend of ours. Six degrees of separation – it is truly a small world. I said that I was on my way to Cuba, because I needed a getaway, but it was bad timing and most of my friends didn't want to get away with me. I told Barb about running the B & B, and how one of our frequent guests had come to visit two weeks before and had mentioned that she needed a getaway, as well. So that night, we had booked the trip and presto! I was meeting her at the airport. When we arrived at my terminal, as I turned to say goodbye, she jumped up and pressed her card into my hand. As I walked away, she poked her head out of the shuttle bus door and yelled, "Judy! The next time you need a travelling buddy, give me a call." I smiled and waved farewell and was still smiling to myself as I entered the airport.

Unfortunately, in the confusion of travelling, I misplaced her card. I always wished that I had given her a call to let her know that our short time together had a lasting impression on me. Yesterday, after writing this section, I got in touch with our shared friends in Niagara Falls, to see if they had her number. They said that she had recently passed away, and they also felt bad that they hadn't gone to visit her. Her zest for life and her kind personality had also touched their hearts.

Barb's flower could be Lavender, which comes in traditional, warm, mauve shades. It's an ancient herb with a delicate scent that has a peaceful effect on those around it.

Sunflowers

Sunflowers remind me of Mark.

They stand tall, with bright yellow happy faces, looking towards the sun.

They help others by spreading their seeds of kindness.

According to Google, "the open face symbolizes the sun itself, conveying warmth, happiness and adoration."

I chose Sunflowers for the cover of this book because my Sunflower, Mark, started me on this entire journey.

A mysterious person used to regularly put a Sunflower on Mark's grave. A Sunflower also reminds me of Jason's pilgrimage to Italy. Jason bought Sarah a bouquet of Sunflowers on their visit there. I hope the Sunflowers on the cover will act as beacons of hope and joy for my readers.

Herb Garden

Thyme   Oregano   Sage   SR.

I choose to remember Jason as an Herb Garden.

He was so passionate, especially about cooking, and always used fresh herbs.

Jason told me he was a healer and herbs have many healing benefits.

He had planned to grow an Herb Garden when he recovered.

My Oak Trees

I couldn't think of a better way to describe my parents. They were loving, strict but fair, and were always there for me. They were very hard workers, but left time for play and fun. When they were married, they moved into their first house. It was probably a shack by today's standards, but it was always neat and tidy. One of the first things Dad did was build Mom a white picket fence in front.

They had played music together since they were teenagers, so our house was often filled with friends playing musical instruments. Mom and Dad would work hard all day in retail stores until they closed at six, and then rush home to quickly eat dinner before going to play at a dance. The band usually came back to our house, where they would keep playing, sometimes until the sun came up. I don't know how they did it – I didn't inherit their energy. The day after each musical celebration, Mom would be up cooking a big Sunday supper in case more company might stop in, to play in the afternoon.

Music washes away from the soul the dust of everyday life.

BERTHOLD AUERBACH

Mom and Dad were always up for a card game, a fishing trip, or a four-wheeler ride together back to Lewisham, where they loved to stay in the hunt camp. They knew how to laugh together. They were soul mates who, as a couple, shared all their friends. I remember when they were planning Dad's surprise retirement party and Mom had to meet with his boss to plan it. Mom said that she hated doing it behind his back; she almost felt as if she were cheating.

Bill and I were married when I was nineteen, so Mom and Dad were empty-nesters when they were only thirty-nine. These days, young couples are just beginning their families at that age.

My parents gave me the gifts of laughter, honesty, kindness, a good work ethic, family pride, high moral standards and most of all, the gift of love. Throughout this book, you have seen some of the thoughtful things my parents have done. One of the times I was most proud of Dad was when he inherited a piece of property from his eldest brother. His other brother, John, was never quite the same with Dad after that, and their relationship changed. John couldn't understand why his brother hadn't left him the property since he was also very close to the older brother. Dad loved the property and talked about building a house on it someday. But he couldn't help worrying about how the property had come between him and John. After thinking about it for a long time, Dad put the property up for sale. When it sold, he divided the money from the sale of the property equally among his remaining siblings. I was proud to be his daughter that day.

Mom never had a big flower garden, but she usually had a nice bed of annuals, kept neatly in front of the house. Her signature flowers were the many bouquets that she purchased to give to anyone who was sick or needed a pick-me-up. She was also known as the card lady, the woman who never missed a birthday, anniversary, or giving a note of caring encouragement when someone was ill. I'm more the well-intentioned woman who thinks that I must send a card, but never gets around to it.

Dad was a gentleman, who always helped little old ladies. He was the kind of guy who everyone called, when they had a problem. He had the mechanical ability to fix things. Children loved him because he knew how to play and always made time for them. Our boys loved their Papa. He had the patience, at Christmas, to put the toys and games together. I realize that I could be describing Mark. They were so much alike, including their propensity for crazy storytelling. Jason took over his music.

When we lost the boys, Mom and Dad and I held each other up. There weren't a lot of tears, but we gave a great deal of caring and strength to each other.

Dad died, from a very sudden heart attack, at the age of eighty-one, in 2009, two years after we lost Jason. I was glad that we had gone on a long-overdue fishing trip, before he passed. The day he died, he had stayed after church to help pack away the hymn books. That's the kind of guy he was.

Mom carried on. I thought she would go to pieces, but not Mom. She had will power and a strong, stubborn streak that would never allow her to quit. Jason took after her in that regard. Mom also had a great sense of humour and loved a good joke, or a card game. She was a hard worker and her church family meant a lot to her and Dad in later years. Her job, in life, seemed to be to worry about everyone and every-thing. We gave her a lot to worry about, over the years, but she always stuck up for Bill. About two weeks before she passed away, she finally moved in with Bill and me. On her last day, she was very weak and I tucked her into bed before supper.

"What are you cooking Bill for supper?" she asked.

"Scalloped potatoes and ham," I answered.

"That's nice."

When I went in to check on her before dessert, she had passed away. Bill response was, "Now who's going to stick up for me?"

Mom and Dad are buried beside the boys with matching grave-stones in Barkway. Bill and I just purchased our matching stone for when we join them.

My Other Oak Tree

This book wouldn't be complete unless I mentioned my other Mighty Oak, my friend BF. He has consistently been there for me. Like a big oak tree, he's sheltered me from many storms and has been a true friend and confidant.

BF always seemed to know when I was having a hard time and would bring a picnic to the doctor's office. We would sit at Bass Rock, or in a quiet park, and have a special "time-out" moment during my lunch hour. He would usually tell me to meditate for five minutes before he would let me eat. Those special times meant the world to me.

Like all good friends, he is hard on me. He is now helping to edit this book and is showing no mercy. A dictionary, one which used to belong to his partner Terry, was his first contribution to help me with my atrocious spelling. He made me look up the meaning of every word I couldn't spell. His next challenge is to make sure I lose some weight and skip the treats. He has a challenge ahead of him, there.

BF and Terry owned a sailboat. Every year, I looked forward to our annual sail on Georgian Bay. They were one of those couples that were easy to be around. This year, BF lost Terry, after a short three-month battle with cancer. Like me, BF is surrounded by a large number of friends. I hope that, in some small way, I can make a difference for him and be there for him the way he has unfailingly been there for me. Thank you, my dear BF.

The Oak Tree

A mighty wind blew night and day.
It stole the oak tree's leaves away.
Then snapped its boughs and pulled its bark,
Until the oak was tired and stark.
But still the oak tree held its ground,
While other trees fell all around.
The weary wind gave up and spoke:
"How can you still be standing, Oak?"
The oak tree said, "I know that you can
break each branch of mine in two,
Carry every leaf away,
Shake my limbs, and make me sway.
But I have roots stretched in the earth,
Growing stronger since my birth.
You'll never touch them, for you see,
They are the deepest part of me.
Until today I wasn't sure
Of just how much I could endure.
But now I've found, with thanks to you,
I'M STRONGER THAN I EVER KNEW"

JOHNNY RAY RYDER JR.

This message came on a card, sent to us after we lost Mark. Like the Oak Tree, I never realized how strong I was. I am thankful for the good root system I received from a wonderful Mom and Dad as well as the other generations before me.

Violets

WILD VIOLET

Violets are the tiny, purple or white, perennials that come out first thing, to announce that spring is here. Our old homestead had plenty of Violets that sprouted up in the lawn and in my flower beds. Some people find they are too invasive, but I enjoyed them. Once they had flowered, I just mowed them with the lawn mower and they became part of my grass until next spring.

Muriel and Joey were two gardening friends who enjoyed playing jokes on each other. Joey gave Muriel some Violets for her garden, but Muriel always complained that they were too invasive. When Muriel died, Joey planted some Violets on her grave. Ironically, the Violets, which normally spread like weeds, stayed in little obedient clumps in the cemetery's sandy soil. They still come up every year to say, "We're still here, and we are behaving, chuckle, chuckle."

Joey got the last laugh. I would be honoured if a friend cared enough about me to take the time to plant flowers on my grave. Friends who have the last laugh have a special way to preserve life, and continue the fun.

When I think of Violets, I think of Grandma Taverner. She didn't grow Violets, but she loved the colour purple. Her bedroom at her farmhouse was adorned with yellow wallpaper covered with purple Violets. I have vivid memories of the first night I spent there, in the Violet room. I was six, and Grandma tucked me into a little cot and pointed to the pretty flowers on the wallpaper. Then she went about her business downstairs.

At first, I was afraid, lying there alone in an unfamiliar room, which was much bigger than any room I'd slept in before. The sloping ceiling and different sounds made me feel scared and alone. Then, I remembered Grandma Taverner talking about the pretty wallpaper. I studied the details of each flower and pattern. Before I knew it, I was sound asleep. What a vivid memory. Imagine all the little children who live each day with fighting parents, or horrible events in their lives. We should all remember how sensitive and impressionable children can be. Thankfully, I am able to focus on my good memories.

Grandma Taverner was a remarkable woman who raised nine children in the early 1900s, in the isolated hamlet of Lewisham, which was located in central Ontario, Canada. She relied on a vegetable garden to help feed her family.

Flowers were a luxury that she could not afford. She had an amazing ability to sing and laugh and make light of life. In her most unhappy times, no one would ever know it. She confided to me that she would often go out to the garden to cut each weed with the hoe, saying, "I hate this place. I hate this place." She said it was a good way to get her garden weeded. She would put her hoe away, go in to make supper for her family and never let on.

Dinners usually consisted of some kind of fish, or wild game, home-made bread, and vegetables from the garden. Grandma had a way of making a small amount of food go a long way. One of her tricks was to fry potatoes and add onions and small squares of bread to make them go further. It was delicious. Once in a while, Bill and I still cook our potatoes that way and remember her.

Grandma was no stranger to hard times. Their first log home burnt to the ground. When it caught fire, her first instinct was to save their most valuable possession – the woodstove. A neighbor saw the smoke and rushed over to help. He and Grandma managed to grab something to protect their hands and carried the stove outside while loaves of bread were still baking in the oven. They didn't even burn their hands.

Grandma was sometimes called upon to deliver babies. She told me a story about a young man who picked her up by buggy in the middle of the night, to help deliver the couple's baby. They were very poor but also very proud. When the baby was born, the young mother wanted to show her gratitude and gave Grandma a tiny meat platter. It was only worth a few pennies, but Grandma valued the dish for the memory. I have the platter now and enjoy telling its story.

Hunting season was always a big deal for the men in the family. I remember the tale of the time Grandpa's brother, George, went out to buy a new pair of overalls for hunting season. In those days, when times were hard, the purchase of a new pair of overalls was a big deal. The night before the season, Grandpa Harold suggested that the overalls would work much better if they were cut off just below the top of his rubber boots. That way, they could walk in water, without getting their overalls wet, but their overalls would still be long enough to keeps leaves and twigs, from falling into the tops of their boots. After a few drinks and a long discussion, they decided it would be a good idea to cut the new pants. The next day, in anticipation of the hunt, they got up before dawn, had an early breakfast, than hurried to put on their overalls. Grandpa's overalls were fine, but George's new ones were the length of shorts. You can imagine the ribbing they took from their fellow hunters. Apparently, George wore his funny overall-shorts for years.

The family farmhouse in Lewisham had three bedrooms that, by today's standards, would be considered quite small. To help with expenses, Grandma rented one of the rooms to the local teacher, so that left only two bedrooms for the eleven members of the family. There were two beds in one room, for the six boys, and the three girls slept in Grandma and Grandpa's room with a sheet strung up for privacy. There was no room for dressers. That didn't matter since they didn't have many clothes.

I never heard any of the children complain about their living conditions. Instead, they grew up as a close family, with great humour and tolerance. Recently, I talked to Uncle Ron, the youngest son. He simply remembered that they had a nice big house to grow up in. I asked how they all fit into the two bedrooms, and he said that it never seemed crowded to him. There always seemed to be lots of room and the body heat came in handy on cold winter nights. They would have to get up very early to keep the woodstove stoked. How things have changed. Now, even Children's Aid requires that children each have their own room. We certainly have created a different society.

I knew my Grandparents in easier times after the Lewisham homesteaders had moved on in search of better lives. My Grandparents' old farmhouse and cabin were sold for a hunting and fishing retreat. They kept one hundred acres for a family hunt camp for their boys and moved about ten miles, to the more accessible and populated farming settlement of Barkway.

After the children were grown, Grandma inherited the Barkway family farm from her parents. That's when I got to spend my weekends visiting her. They were my fun Grandparents. One of my fondest memories was accompanying Grandma into the garden, where she filled her apron with peas. Together, we sat on the grass, shelling peas, eating some of them and laughing together. Grandma said we were like two peas in a pod. She was right.

Grandpa never grew up and still enjoyed life at ninety. He always had a crokinole board set up in his basement for all the neighbourhood kids who would stop in for a game. He loved to fish, hunt, step dance and play crokinole and cards. He once made us each a pair of stilts. We used them to walk up the road, about a hundred yards, to the Rebman's, who were my other Grandparents. It was a fair distance on stilts.

Grandpa drove an old tractor-like Jeep called Nelly. It had a Model-T engine, set on a frame, with tractor tires. There was one seat for the driver, and a spot beside it, with a cushion on top of a bunch of chains. Neighbours often saw us going fishing in Old Nelly. We would rumble and rattle down the road with wooden poles sticking out the back. I would be sitting on the cushion, bouncing up and down and holding on for dear life.

Grandpa loved to go for long walks every day, which probably contributed to his good health.

Gladiolas

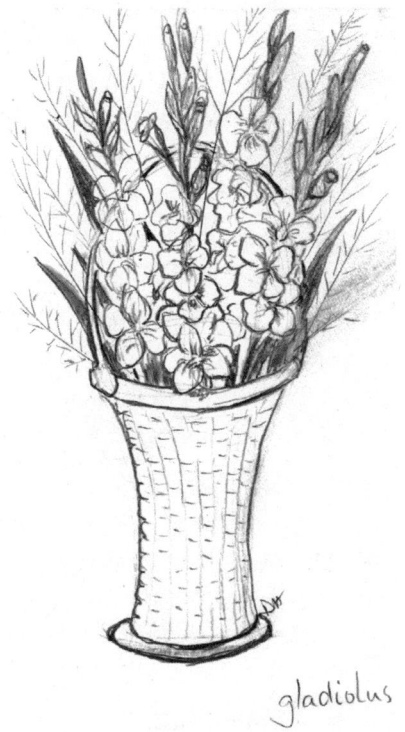

gladiolus

Gladiolas are a very popular cut flower. A lot of pioneer women planted them around their vegetable gardens, probably because they do well in rows, and are easier to weed. I like to think that seeing the vibrant colours of the Gladiolas also gave those women some joy, while they were busy bringing in their fall harvest.

My Grandmother Rebman was one of those pioneer women; she was a remarkable self-starter. Gladiolas remind me of her because, every Sunday, she would proudly make up a bouquet of flowers for the Sunday church service. She had an artistic side and her flower arrangements always had a tasteful charm. My favourite arrangements were made up of Gladiolas and asparagus ferns, arranged in two white antique baskets. I must have taken after her because I have enjoyed making arrangements for our little country summer church. Maybe she helped contribute to my love of gardening. My Grandma took pride in her flower gardens and her two large vegetable plots. As a child, it seemed like too much work to me. I still have a memory of Grandma, with her terrible, arthritic, twisted legs bent over for hours weeding her gardens, in the hot sun. For her, weeding was a matter of pride and perhaps guilt, since she needed the garden to feed her family.

Grandma always found time to write. She was interested in preserving history, and helped compose the Women's Institute's Tweedsmuir history. She wrote a weekly news column, "The Barkway News," for the local newspaper. I share her love of writing and her sense of history. That is why I am writing this book. Grandma's daughter-in-law has followed in her footsteps, as well, and has continued compiling the facts about the history of our family and the community of Barkway. Without realizing it, Grandma was making an impression on us by setting a good example. This is all the more reason to think about the example we are setting for our loved ones and peers.

Running a farm was a lot of work for my Grandparents. They had to get up at 5:30 a.m., seven days a week, to milk the dairy cows. They had to milk again at 4:30 p.m. Life was difficult, but as children, we always enjoyed helping out with chores: gathering eggs, bringing home the cows from pasture to be milked and bringing in the hay. We always felt loved, but it was a strict, regimental, busy-life kind of love. Grandma and Grandpa Rebman always had a garden of responsibilities.

When the time came to sell the farm, Grandma and Grandpa accepted it amazingly well. They just saw it as another stage of life. They had done a fine job and it was their turn to go out to pasture. I think they were relieved that there were no more chores to be done. Ironically, when the farm was sold, the gardens and the busy farm life soon disappeared. Horses now run where dairy herds had pastured before. Weeds and grass grow where the large family gardens flourished.

Dahlias

Dahlia

Dahlias come in all shapes and bright shades. The bulbs can be quite expensive and usually come one or two in a package. They are planted in spring, and then removed in fall, before the first frost. Each year that Dahlias flower, the bulbs will multiply. If you store the bulbs properly, and divide them in the spring before replanting, you will soon have a nice showing of Dahlias in your garden. Storage is a problem for me. They usually either dry out, or go mouldy and rot.

Dahlias were Marg's pride and joy. My mother-in-law especially loved mauve ones. She lived in an old farmhouse and had a cellar, which is the perfect place to store them. Over the years, she often shared her bulbs with me.

Marg took pride in her children, her farm (especially her cattle) and her pies and butter tarts. She was a fun Grandmother, who loved to play cards and shop. She was a hard worker who would cook a meal for everyone, then put on her work pants and go to the barn to do the chores and feed the cattle. She allowed her boys to help, but she would have to be there to supervise. She always stressed the importance of keeping the family unit free from outside influences. She also stressed to her family the importance of keeping the family farm. Her parents gave it to them as a wedding present. This often caused problems in their marriage because she felt it was hers, not theirs.

Poor Marg dreamed she would get her old-age pension, but unfortunately, she passed away just before she received her first cheque. The old farmhouse burned down shortly after she died, and without her strong influence the family members became estranged from each other. Ironically, the land and sibling jealousy have been the main factors in that estrangement.

Bill considered himself the black sheep of the family because he never followed the rules. He enjoyed outside influences, and as the third son, was often told he could never do things on the farm as well as his older brothers. He lost interest and his self-confidence. He never inherited any of the family property, or the responsibilities that went along with the homestead. He didn't gain much financially, but I think in the long run he was the winner.

I guess you could compare the family to Dahlia bulbs that were not looked after or stored properly. The family, as Marg remembered it, will never bloom again. Her Dahlias at the homestead are lost forever. I loved Marg, but I didn't agree with her philosophy of keeping the family together without outside influences. Family is very important to me, but I believe you should also make time for friends and interests, outside the family. Being open to other points of view makes you a more rounded and interesting person, one who is less prejudiced and less rigid in your thinking. If I had had brothers and sisters, I might have a different philosophy, but I was an only child who loved people and had outgoing parents. Dad's example of selling his property for his brothers and sisters gave me a better example to follow. Now that I have lost my children, I thank goodness that I have my outside interests and special friends. Without them I could have become a shriveled up old Dahlia bulb!

Nasturtiums

Nasturtiums

I had my first gardening experience when I was about six. Mom bought a package of Nasturtium seeds and helped me to plant them. As we were planting them, she explained that Nasturtiums were my Great-Grandmother's favourite flowers. We would watch them grow together. I was shocked when they actually did grow. This was such a nice experience with Mom. Now, I like to plant some Nasturtiums to preserve the memory.

Great Grandmother was a smart lady to like Nasturtiums, which is an annual that flourishes even in poor soil. They are hardy plants that keep blooming all summer, right up until the first frost.

I have seen them planted in window boxes, and they make a nice showing for a reasonable price. The flowers, and leaves of Nasturtiums are edible, and have a somewhat peppery taste. When we operated the bed and breakfast, they were great for garnishing breakfast dishes. I must admit that, over the years, only three guests were adventurous enough to actually eat the flowers. I remember when I visited my girlfriend Pam in England, she didn't have quite enough greens for the salad so she went out to her garden and added some Nasturtium leaves. They were quite tasty.

Phlox

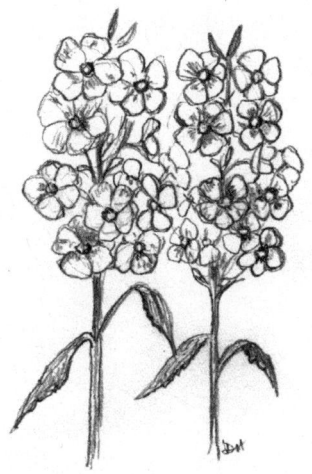

Phlox are a wonderful bright addition to the perennial garden. When all the other flowers have begun to fade, the Phlox come out to shine. They make a nice showing when planted with Black-eyed Susans (Rudbeckia), Coneflowers, and Sedum. These are all fall flowers that bloom around the same time.

There is also a type of wild Phlox that comes out in the spring. It's wonderful to see some colour peeking through the bush, on the edge of our property. They come up in the strangest places, without any helping hand from me, something like children who have been left to fend for themselves who still manage to find a spot to shine.

In my Memory Garden, I have a bright pink Phlox in memory of my Dad's Grandparents. They were homesteaders in the 1800s in Lewisham. A few years ago, Dad bought the homestead property. It's now dense bush and no one would ever know that anyone had ever had a home, let alone raised a family there. One day, Dad was riding his four-wheeler through the property and he saw a bright colour shining through the bush. He rode over to it, and found some pink Phlox sending out a signal that someone had taken the time to plant them over a hundred years before, and that they had survived to carry on the memory. Maybe we could learn from this that even the tiny things we do in life can make a difference to others and ourselves, be it a good thing or a bad thing. We must focus on those significant moments.

Marigolds

I plant Marigolds for their vibrant yellow and orange colours. Marigolds are great annual flowers that add long-lasting colour to a flower garden. Once you get them established and keep them watered and dead-headed, they will give a good showing until the first frost. Their very distinct smell helps discourage our local deer. Unfortunately, it doesn't always work – I still see deer standing in the middle of the Marigolds, eating everything except the Marigolds.

In my Memory Garden, Marigolds remind me of my Aunt Eileen Hess (Taverner). She was an amazing woman, the oldest of nine children, who ended up looking after her mother, father, husband, daughter, and her granddaughter. Everyone depended on her. She was a beautiful, proud, organized woman who took pride in her appearance and loved to cook, sew and garden. She also took pride in her home, decorating it with a simple sophisticated elegance that mirrored her own flair. She lived on a small lake, and showed her artistic ability in her gardens, creating paths around the birch trees, surrounding them with a variety of vegetables, Marigolds, Impatiens, and other flowers.

Aunt Eileen passed away in her nineties. For over ten years, she suffered from Alzheimer's disease and lived in a nursing home. It is so unfair that she suffered a life sentence as the shell of the woman she had been. How could such a vibrant person end her life this way? It makes me sad whenever I think of her. Getting Alzheimer's is my greatest fear. It is a horrible disease that wreaks havoc on the patient as well as on caregivers. By the time the patient finally does pass away, he or she is a stranger to the family. There is nothing worse than not being recognized by someone who you love.

Pansies

Pansies are among my favourite annual flowers. They come in a variety of vivid mixed colours, with tiny smiling faces that welcome spring. My Aunt Arla plants Pansies in two large blue ceramic containers outside her home. To me, that bunch of bright, colourful, happy Pansies dancing in the sunlight resembles Aunt Arla's family.

Arla and I have always had a bond that is strengthened by mutual respect and admiration. Maybe we were sisters in a past life. We are both only children who have learned to appreciate the importance of family. We also share the same ideals and interests which include: an appreciation for the outdoors, travelling, shopping, playing cards, dancing and good food. Did I mention that we both have a weight problem? She doesn't share my passion for gardening, largely because she hasn't had as many troubles to dig through. Arla doesn't have time to garden because she is too busy living life to the fullest.

I love her philosophy of life and some terrific sayings. To Aunt Arla, "Someday is now." The purpose of marriage is: "You always have a Saturday night date."

Another one of her favorite rules is: "When someone takes the time to plan a party, it is your job to go and have a good time."

If someone asks her opinion, she always gives an honest answer, even if the person on the other end doesn't like the response. Whenever I was going through a rough patch, I knew I could always depend on Aunt Arla to take the time to listen carefully to my problems and to give me her honest advice. I didn't always follow her advice, but I always respected what she had to say, and considered it carefully before I made a decision.

Arla and her husband Aubrey got together when their two horse-trading fathers arranged their first date. I don't think any livestock or money changed hands, but apparently it proved to be a good deal. They were a well-matched team; they will have been hitched for sixty years in 2015. Because of their upbringing, horses have always played an important role in their lives. When they were first married, they decided to hitch up a horse and cutter to go for a Sunday drive down their street. They waved proudly to all the neighbours, as their well-groomed horse trotted gallantly past each home.

Apparently, something happened at the end of the block. The next thing the neighbours saw was Aubrey pulling the cutter, and Arla leading the horse back to the barn. We all love that story. They still enjoy going to fairs to watch the horse shows. At their home fair, you will probably find Arla in the fair booth announcing the events.

Here, according to Arla, are some of the secrets to their successful marriage: always respect each other, share similar interests, agree on high morals, work hard, play often and always keep a sense of humour. Over the years, Arla has learned the knack of getting her own way, while letting Aubrey think it was his idea. Aubrey has always been a worrier, but they have learned to work together, to solve every problem that arises. They have raised three daughters who are their pride and joy. From the very beginning, they took parenthood very seriously.

Arla has always hugged her children (and me) and says, "I love you, I love you." Arla and Aubrey taught their children by example, so the girls always knew what was important.

Their church congregation has meant a lot to their family. I still remember Uncle Aubrey helping his girls get ready for Sunday school by doing up their dresses, braiding their hair, putting in hair clips and tying their shoes. There were often tears but he had a little trick to make them feel better.

"Blow your nose to make it all better," he would say, handing out a hanky.

Have you ever tried to cry and blow your nose at the same time? It's impossible. The girls learned to dance by dancing with their parents, to the music from Don Messer's Jubilee. They all still love to dance.

The Rebmans have a wonderful circle of friends. They have taught their daughters the importance and value, of friendship.

Both Arla and Aubrey played an active role in raising their family. They believed that the family which plays together stays together and they were right. Arla taught her girls the saying "unto yourself be true." This came in handy when they began their university years. For Aubrey, sending his girls to university was worth every penny, not only for the knowledge, and good jobs they received, but more importantly, because of the good husbands they met, the lifelong friends they made and the confident, hard-working, open-minded individuals they became.

Arla and Aubrey love to travel and their girls have followed in their footsteps. They've also continued their quest for fun by purchasing a cottage on Wood Lake. Now, in true Rebman form, two of their daughters have also purchased cottages on the lake. The cottages are always a beehive of excitement and activities. Music plays an important role, as the sons-in-law have a band. The grandchildren all love to sing and play, as well.

I have often been envious of the busy, crazy, loving, successful, emotional, musical, fun-loving Rebman family. They all realize how lucky they are and value what they have. They have been lucky, but they have also been blessed with a good root system, with two special parents who have kept their family garden-healthy by nurturing them with dependable, consistent, strict love. The next time you see a patch of Pansies, think of Arla's philosophies of life.

Poppies

When I see a Poppy, I remember "Uncle Tav." His real name was Lawrence but Tav (short for Taverner) was his Army nickname. Uncle Tav was a sniper in World War II, which was one of the most dangerous assignments. He was probably chosen for that task because he was such a good marksman. Growing up in Lewisham, wild game had been his family's staple diet. I remember an old picture that Grandma had of Tav, surrounded by children overseas, during the war. Apparently he would sneak behind enemy lines to steal food and blankets for the little ones. He was just that kind of guy. He had a big, soft heart and loved kids.

Tav was thankful to have survived the war. While on a mission, he stepped out from behind a brick wall and was caught in machine-gun fire. One bullet pierced his shoulder while a second ricocheted off the wall and lodged between his eyes. His entire body was peppered with shrapnel fragments. The next thing he remembered was hearing a doctor tell him that he was a lucky guy; they had just removed a bullet from between his eyes! Unfortunately the doctors were unable to remove the bullet from his shoulder because of its location.

Tav survived, but the war took its toll on him. He suffered from terrible headaches. When the bullet in his shoulder moved to a critical area, it caused him pain and other problems. Years after the war, you could still see pieces of shrapnel in the bottom of the tub after he had a bath. Every time he travelled, he had a hard time getting through airport security.

Shortly after Tav came home from the war, he married Eileen. They had many good times during their marriage, but it's a shame they never had any children. Tav and Eileen did help raise their nephew, who became as close to them as a son.

Tav was soft-hearted throughout his life. He often helped neighbourhood kids who were in trouble. His home was always open to them, if they needed a place to stay. As the saying goes, "Tav would give you the shirt off his back." His concern also extended to older people. One older woman thought of him as a son and looked forward to his visits.

He was also a fun uncle to my cousins and me. I have very fond memories of going to their family cottage. We rode there in an old Model-T Ford that Uncle Tav had fixed up for the rough road. I remember laughing with my cousins, as we bounced up and down in the back seat. He took us fishing every day and my cousins and I spent all week making a raft out of fallen logs. We couldn't wait for the big launch and everyone helped carry our pride and joy down to the lake.

The launch went fine, but Uncle Tav thought he should take it out for the maiden voyage. We eagerly watched as he pushed the raft out into the water before he climbed aboard. He stood tall and saluted us, as we all cheered with glee. Suddenly, the raft began to sink. Tav held his position, saluting and singing the national anthem, until it sunk like a stone. The only evidence of Uncle Tav was bubbles, which appeared where the raft had floated moments before. Tav came back up to the surface and we all roared with laughter. You can't beat those kinds of childhood memories.

Uncle Tav always spoke loudly because of his hearing loss. He would come into a room and either yodel, or make a joke. He was a big, well-meaning guy, who had a lot of pain and physical problems to endure. Unfortunately, he would often have a bit too much to drink.

While overseas, Uncle Tav longed for home and his bride. In his haste to get home, he signed his release papers before arranging for a pension for himself. Uncle Tav paid dearly for that mistake. Near the end of his life, he was only getting about fifty dollars per month, and the Royal Canadian Legion fought hard to get him more money. My Aunt told us that he did get a small raise before he died.

He never spoke about the war to us kids. The only thing he did tell us was not to be prejudiced, because the war was over.

Uncle Tav was another hero who truly made a difference in my life.

Wild Roses

I was recently travelling in Alaska and noticed some Wild Roses growing beside the road. Wild Roses often appear randomly beside abandoned fields, displaying their natural beauty.

For some reason, when I think about Wild Roses, I think of our good friend, Shad.

Shad loved the Wild Roses that grew easily on his family property. They were a reminder of the pioneers who had come before. I think he liked them because they symbolized how he wanted to live his life, wild and free, without giving up his well-rooted family beginnings. Like the Wild Rose, he didn't fit into a cultured flower bed and he also didn't venture very far from his roots.

I first met Shad when he was young and free; he was a rebel without a cause. He was a tall, lanky, good-looking truck-driving kid who used to stop in at my parents' house. Dad helped him learn to play the guitar. Shad was happiest when he was singing, playing music and hanging out with friends. His nicknames were The Legend, Tex and Big Guy. His love of history and storytelling led him to write many songs that his sons still sing today. Shad was the lead singer in my parents' band when they played at the Hunters' Club dances in the 1950s. "Fraulein" was their theme song. Around that time, he would sometimes get me to sit on Mom's piano bench and sing *As I Was Slowly Passing*, a sad old country song. For years, he carried my toothless picture in his wallet. He had a way of making you feel special and I told Mom and Dad that I was going to marry him when I grew up. Unfortunately, Dawn beat me to the draw. Dawn was made for Shad, the perfect woman for him. Shad was not an easy man to be married to, but Dawn was a wife with class and dignity. She still is one of the strongest people I know.

Over the years, Shad woke Mom and Dad up in the middle of night on several occasions, when he brought friends over to play music. When Shad and Dawn got married, Mom and Dad got even and staged a chivaree – a noisy mock serenade of a newly-married couple – on their wedding night, at Dawn's family cottage.

As soon as Shad and Dawn got married, he became a family man. He worked hard to make a home and took pride in his new family. He had two sons, and a daughter whom he nicknamed Sweet Thang. A Sweet Thang she was, and always will be. He passed his music on to his children. His boys sang in a band together and the oldest son has won several singing awards. I love hearing his boys sing harmony.

Shad was the master of ceremonies at our wedding and he and Dawn have always played an important role in our family history. Unfortunately, a few years ago, we noticed a change in Shad. Dawn kept him at home as long as she possibly could, but his dementia became too advanced for even a strong woman like Dawn to handle. Shad is now in a nursing home and has adjusted quite well. The love of his life visits him faithfully, every day.

Bill and I recently visited the Alamo in San Antonio, Texas. The Alamo touched my heart and I thought of all the American heroes who lost their lives fighting in the Texas Revolution, for Texas independence – heroes like Davey Crockett and Daniel Boone. In the courtyard, next to an old stone building, I noticed a lovely Wild Rose growing and couldn't help thinking of my buddy Shad.

His first great grandson "Jack" was just christened in the final service of the old Harmony Corner's United church. Although Shad wasn't there, Dawn was beaming while surrounded by their beautiful family. From the humble beginning of a wild rose, a wonderful legacy was created.

Sweet Williams

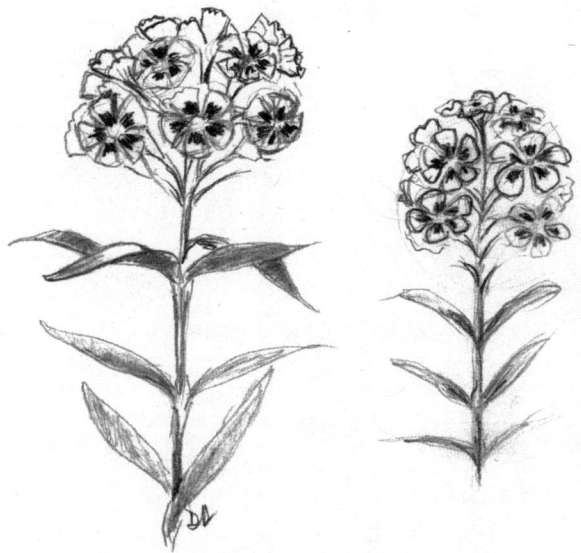

Sweet Williams remind me of a grumpy old guy, Joe, who lived his whole life without getting the real meaning of life. Joe and his wife lived next door to my office. His house was the one with the large "No Turning" sign in the driveway. On my way into work, whenever Joe was working in his yard, I would often say hello or stop for a chat.

Joe loved to garden and I would sometimes ask him for pointers or admire his flowers. The flowers were very healthy because he was always fertilizing or spraying for pests. But it was hard to enjoy the ambiance of his flowers because they were often surrounded with small, electric, wire fences, other kinds of barricades, or animal traps.

219

If you were a squirrel, raccoon, or other varmint, you didn't mess with Joe's garden.

The Sweet Williams seemed to grow naturally for him. From our office window, we could see a bright red and deep pink bed beside his garage. I liked this garden the most because it didn't have any protective fences and it seemed to shine without much help from Joe. Roses were Joe's particular pride and joy. He would often give me a special one to put on my desk.

When his wife got ill and went to live with their daughter, I would sometimes take him out for lunch. He was the same age as my Grandfather and I felt sorry for him because I knew he was lonely. At first, I enjoyed his stories of growing up and raising his family, but I couldn't help but notice that he never asked me about my family even though he knew I had lost my son. As time went on, I noticed a change in his demeanor. All Joe could talk about was how everyone cheated him, owed him money, or took advantage of him. It was always the same stories, over and over again. His neighbours were very good to him but he turned against them. His two children seemed very angry with him. When another woman, about my age, also felt sorry for him, and offered to clean his house, he accused her of stealing from him and not doing a very good job. He didn't understand why she was upset.

Unfortunately, Joe took my friendliness too seriously. He would often be waiting outside for me, before and after work. He seemed to have a crush on me and started calling me at home. I became very tired of his negativity and pestering. I began to avoid him, in hopes he would get the message. Then, when Joe's wife died, I saw a picture of her as a young woman, and immediately saw a resemblance to me. I think Joe was drawn to me because I reminded him of their younger years. It was so sad because he seemed to turn everyone against him and felt wronged by everyone around him. Perhaps he was developing early dementia.

Over the years, Joe gave me a few different plants for my garden. I put them together in a section, in remembrance of him. Some people seem to go through life not being able to see the forest for the trees.

They are so absorbed with their own perceived grievances and take life so seriously, that they end up missing so much of life. If they could learn to laugh at themselves, to be more forgiving and accepting of others, they would gain so much in return.

So the next time you see some Sweet Williams, remember to be sweet, not sour like Joe.

Be Better Not Bitter

Orchids

Orchid

Most of this book's illustrations and the wonderful sketch of Mark standing in his firefighting gear, beside his old blue truck, were done by another hero, Dorothy Hillman. I think she brought Mark to life; she certainly captured his wonderful smile.

Dorothy has the smile of an Angel and sings like a bird. I love to see her bombing around on the little red scooter she has named Ruby. The back bumper plate says, "Don't take your love to town." She and her partner, Tom, are always laughing and enjoying life together. Tom is her roadie and her sous chef, who always looks after Dorothy's needs. Tom's eyesight is failing, so Dorothy has read him more than one hundred books, imitating each character's voice as she reads. They are soul mates who are better together than apart.

No one would guess that Dorothy's bones are very porous and her body is completely riddled with rheumatoid arthritis. She has had numerous surgeries and her hands are terribly twisted out of shape. It amazes me how she can paint and draw such detailed and life-like pictures. Dorothy makes light of her afflictions and is thankful for her many gifts. I feel blessed to know her, to receive her gifts of joy and I try to follow the example she sets. It makes me want to be better in my own life.

Dorothy is an Orchid in my Memory Garden. Orchids are so rare, delicate, fragile and hard to grow, yet they bring the world so much pleasure with their beauty.

Love is a friendship set to Music.

JOSEPH CAMPBELL

Cleomes

Cleomes remind me of my good friend Carol, with whom I share a love of gardening.

Carol always had a wonderful showing of Cleomes in her garden at her family homestead she called Wits End B & B. Most people have trouble growing these special flowers, but Carol's plants seeded themselves and came up like weeds in her garden.

Her gardens were always more artistic than mine because she wasn't afraid to learn or take a chance on trying new things. She turned a large front pasture section of her property into a garden by trying a "lasagna" type of design. First, you cover the grass with newspapers, then leaves and finally soil. The grass on the bottom decays and improves the soil, while the newspapers keep the weeds from coming through. It's like having the benefit of compost while creating a new garden at the same time. Carol mastered this method and her garden thrived – especially her Cleomes.

Carol and I have a lot of things in common. We both grew up in the same area and cherish the love of family and country living. I have a fond memory of Carol and me swimming across Doe Lake as teenagers, with Dad by our side, rowing the boat. I felt like a young Marilyn Bell.

She's a few years older than I am and when we rode on the school bus together, I looked up to her and thought she was so much wiser and more grownup than me. I still think she is so much wiser and still admire her abilities. She is helping me with the layout of this book and has an amazing talent for placing pictures and adding her own special touches.

I hadn't seen Carol for a few years but we renewed our friendship when we each ran a B & B. Carol became my mentor. She taught me many tricks and helped us get the B & B off the ground. She and her partner Mike were very active in the Muskoka B & B Association. Of course, Carol could never do things halfway and got very involved in helping the association design its brochure and the website. She is also a talented photographer. The four of us like playing cards and enjoy many laughs during a good game of Euchre. I think the boys are ahead at the moment, but we girls plan to change that the next time we play.

Sadly, Carol and I have something else in common; we have both lost children to cancer, two months apart. Jason was in the middle of his battle when Carol's daughter Ruthie was suspected of having the disease as well. Carol called me to ask for help. How could she deal with this? What would she have to do? What could she expect next? I told her about my boxes and just gave her my love and support. My heart went out to her. Ruthie died a week later in Carol's arms.

Carol and I also lost the first loves of our lives, our Dads, very soon after losing our children. After that, my Carol lost her luster and part of her wonderful spark was extinguished. She seemed to lose interest in gardening and the B & B. They sold their B & B, just as we did, and have renovated a new residence, just as we did.

She and Mike have also begun to travel. Their first mission was to take some of Ruthie's ashes across Canada and up to the Yukon where her son lives. They sprinkled them in special spots along their journey. At the same time, they were able to spend some quality time with their son. When we lose a child, we cherish our other children even more and value our moments together. That holiday played an important part in Carol's healing.

It's hard to keep a good woman down. After some time, the old Carol came back to us and her wonderful smile came shining through, once more. She just spent a year developing a four-disc series celebrating the history of Ryde Township. This DVD collection is very professionally done and should be a feather in one of her many caps. The project was also another important part of Carol's journey because it gave her a purpose, and made her feel as if she were making a difference for her community. While making the DVD, she also came to admire our pioneer forefathers and appreciate the hardships and struggles, they overcame. Maybe this helped her overcome her hardships as well. It is another example of helping ourselves while we help others.

Last week, when I drove past Carol's old homestead, where they ran the B & B, I couldn't help but notice that the old white farmhouse was still nestled in an abundance of flowers. All of Carol's hard work, to establish these wonderful gardens, had not been in vain.

We are both in the midst of our life journeys and I am glad we have each other with whom to travel.

The photograph of the cleomes above was taken by Carol.

Weeds

My garden wouldn't be complete without mentioning the pesky weeds. Weeds can have underground runners that allow them to spread quickly, or deep roots that become imbedded and become difficult to pull out.

Weeds, in my garden, could represent dealing with death and bad experiences in our lives.

Steve was a young man who grew up with an alcoholic stepdad. The stepdad wasn't physically abusive, but he was still hard on Steve, always putting him down when he failed. Steve wasn't going to amount to anything, according to his stepdad. Sure enough, after Steve left home, he turned out exactly the way his stepdad had predicted.

One day, I met up with Steve and noticed he had an injured hand. Steve told me he had gotten drunk and went into a rage about his stepdad. He had smashed his hand against a cement wall. He said he hated his stepdad and blamed him for the injured hand. He also blamed him because his life wasn't going well. Steve's weeds of hate, insecurity and anger were deeply embedded and began to take over his "successful life" garden.

I felt empathy for Steve, but knew that he was also using the stepdad's behaviour as an excuse. I tried to explain that he had to live a better life for himself and prove the stepdad was wrong about him. If he kept living the way he was living, I reasoned, the stepdad would be the winner.

In the same way, if we let grief and death consume us, then death wins. Isn't it better for "life" to win?

The Tiger Lily

Tiger Lily

I first met Dave when he planned a fund raiser for my son Jason. Dave is the type of guy who sees a need and does something about it.

Jason and Dave were drawn together because of their love for music. Dave was a drummer for the band "Soil" and Jay played lead guitar. Jay joined the band when the former lead guitarist moved to Toronto. Dave said he was impressed that Jason learned twenty-six songs in less than two weeks.

As for Dave, his drumming career began when he was three and banged away on the Salvation Army base drum. His mother was a

Sunday School teacher and also worked at an old-age home. Dave remembers being very young when his mom harmonized with his sister and himself when they sang to entertain the patients at the home. Without realizing it, Dave was learning compassion.

Unfortunately, Dave didn't have it easy growing up. Money was tight and his stepdad had a disability and a drinking problem. When he drank, he became both verbally and physically abusive, especially towards Dave's Mom. When Dave turned twelve, his life changed course. After a very traumatic, brutal experience, his mom finally left the marriage.

During a high-school romance, Dave became a father at the age of eighteen. They didn't get married, but his girlfriend kept their daughter and Dave kept in touch. Unfortunately, the day after she turned nineteen, his daughter was killed from a snowmobile accident. Like myself, Dave experienced grief.

In spite of his shaky beginnings, Dave became an ophthalmic technician and was well respected where he worked.

Martial Arts became an important part of Dave's life in his twenties and he soon learned discipline, strength, concentration and control. He discovered he had an ability and a passion for teaching and began instructing a taekwondo class in his mid-thirties at his sister Wendy's "Just 4 Kicks" studio. Bad luck seemed to follow Dave and while he was training in martial arts 2011, he felt a tingle in his neck and was unaware that it was a severe injury to his carotid artery. Later, he returned home, went to sleep and woke up two hours later in the night and couldn't move. Dave had had two consecutive strokes and was told he would probably never walk normally again. His determination kicked in and Dave spent hours trying to concentrate on getting one finger to move. When he conquered that, he would move forward to the next. After months of therapy Dave learned to walk again.

I recall two times that Dave pulled on my heart strings. The first was during the Christmas get-to-gather after we lost Jay. He came out with the gang on the bus and not only had a part in my special gift from the Acrimony Band but also presented me with another thoughtful gift of a small thyme Christmas tree. This was significant because of Jason's love for cooking. The second time was during a fundraiser for Dave. He stood up to thank everyone and struggled to keep his balance as he held his cane and bravely and sincerely sang "Imagine" by John Lennon.

It is now four years since Dave's stroke. He still has some impairment, but it has not quelled his passion to teach. Four nights a week, you will find Dave teaching his students taekwondo. He feels that in some ways his disability has made him a somewhat better teacher who is more observant, patient and more focused on details of the bio mechanics of the student's movement. While he is helping his students, he is improving his own agility, discipline and creativity. It is a win-win situation.

Dave had even more adversities than Steve in my "weeds section." Fortunately, he chose the higher ground and changed the cycle of history by doing something positive. Over the years, not like Steve, Dave came to terms with his stepdad and was able to forgive him.

His stepdad became a better person and died a hero. He went back into a burning building to save another disabled person and sadly they both were overtaken with the smoke and perished.

The Tiger Lily grows in the shape of a star, which is Dave. It symbolises courage, pride, protection that he teaches his students, and wealth. I doubt if Dave will ever be rich but it is his richness of spirt that counts.

Dave is one of my special boys. He has touched my heart and brought me joy. He knows I am cheering him on.

Gardens in my Mind

When I think of all the friends and family who have played important roles along my journey, I see them as gardens in my memory.

Our "Lake of Bays Neighbour Garden" will always be an important part of my own Memory Garden. Over the years, they have always been there during our trials, losses and successes. They have been a supportive, and fun group who have shared with us many "happy hours," during which we laughed at life's problems. When we needed a helping hand, they were always there.

My "Archdekin Clinic Family Garden" kept me alive, while we worked together helping others. We worked together, as a team, and that gave me purpose and support. Above all, they kept me real. We would have serious discussions about life one minute, then end up laughing at ourselves the next. Being surrounded by other people's illness, we learned never to take ourselves too seriously. I was always easy prey, which amused the girls. One time, I came back from lunch, after a quick trip to the Salvation Army Thrift Store, with my blouse inside out. I didn't realize it, until a patient pointed it out.

My "Patients Garden" became another extended family. They helped me through my troubles, while I was helping them with theirs. When you lose a loved one, you become more aware, and are better understanding of the needs, and emotions, of others. I found a little hug, or a kind ear, made a big difference in their battles. At the end of the day, we all felt better.

My "Pioneer Garden" is full of the friends and family who paved the road to Barkway. They form part of my heritage; they are the roots. They helped shape me into the person I have become. Together, we have shared life together over the years.

My "Aunts and Uncles Garden" has given me the gift of love and laughter all my life. They set high standards for me to follow and gave me good examples to emulate. I will be eternally grateful. I know that those beginnings in life have helped chart my path, have helped me to not give up, and to keep trying my best to succeed.

My "Cousins Garden" is made up of a talented group of honest, hardworking individuals. Thanks for the memories. We made our parents proud.

The "Nieces and Nephews Garden" is important to me. You are my hope for the future. May your gardens be happy ones that grow strong, healthy and successful.

The "Friends of Jason and Mark Garden" is my feel-good garden. You are also my hope for the future and I wish you peace and happiness. I know some of you have had a hard garden to till, but know that I have faith in you all. May you learn from my sons' examples and know that you mean the world to me. Thank you for being there for Bill and me whenever we needed to feel close to our sons.

Our "Marriage Garden" has had a lot of rocky parts. It is a nice piece of land, but it is full of boulders, thin soil and a lot of weeds. It has taken a lot of work to clear the stones, add new soil in the form of friendships, as well as the compost of learning new things, patience and caring. At the moment, our crop is doing quite well.

When I die, I would like to be remembered as a colourful "Country Garden" representing my wonderful friends and family who have helped me become myself.

MEMORIES

Christmas Memories

Although Bill and I have started a new tradition of skipping Christmas, I still have many special memories. To continue the gift of my family roots, I have added a couple of my favourite family Christmas stories that will remain with me always.

There Is a Santa Claus

My Taverner Grandparents were pioneers who raised nine children on a rocky, barren and unforgiving homestead in Lewisham. They had to depend on wild game, fish, berries, and a large vegetable garden to sustain them. Grandpa Harold supplemented their income with seasonal work in logging camps and by guiding hunters and fisherman.

One Christmas, they were going through harder times than usual and had absolutely nothing to give their children. Grandma's faith was being tested, so when she was baking some cookies for her children, she prayed for a miracle. On Christmas Eve, in desperation, she asked Grandpa to hitch up the team and sleigh and go to the Barkway General Store to purchase some fruit or candies for the children's stockings. He began the ten-mile trek, facing the bitter cold and cutting winds as the horses waded in snow past their knees. It was a relief to hear the familiar ring of the store's entrance bell as he came in out of the cold. Grandpa began shaking the snow and frost off his hat and boots and was still clearing the frost from his glasses, when the storekeeper gave him with a hearty greeting.

"Merry Christmas, Harold. I'm surprised to see you out on such a blustery day. Have you come to pick up the very large parcel that was delivered for your family?"

"What parcel?" Harold asked. "We didn't order anything."

The storekeeper presented Grandpa with the mysterious parcel. It was quite bulky, and was wrapped in plain brown paper that was secured by twine. He puzzled over it all the way home. As soon as the horses were safely tied in their stalls and fed and watered, he unloaded the precious cargo and ran into the house to rip it open. Inside, he and Grandma found a special gift for all nine children. It had been sent by one of the fisherman who had hired Grandpa as a guide the previous summer.

The gift my Dad, Jim Taverner, received was a tiny yellow-and-red tin violin with wire strings and tuning pegs that even turned. He spent weeks trying to make the strings play a tune. This little violin sparked a love of music in my Dad that continued the rest of his life. He played violin, guitar and banjo for dances, from the age of fifteen until he was nearly eighty. Dad always said that the long-ago Christmas when he received his violin was one of the best he ever had. I still hang a tiny violin on my Christmas tree to remind myself of that special time. Grandmother believed in Santa until the day she died.

In the Garden

In the Garden has always been a special hymn for both the Rebmans and Taverners. It has often been sung for family funerals, and will be sung at my own when my time comes.

Both sets of grandparents loved to sing.

My Dad and his brother John, both married Rebman sisters, which made the cousins very close. We shared four Grandparents who lived only yards apart in Barkway. .

Christmas, growing up, was wonderful. With me being an only child, our little family would get up early, open our presents, and head to Barkway for lunch with the Taverner family. Along the way, Mom and Dad would always have to make a couple of stops at the homes of lonely, elderly, people to give each a little gift and spread a little Christmas cheer. This taught me the real meaning of Christmas.

When we reached Barkway, the real fun began. The Taverner house was a flurry of activity with Grandma cooking up a feast and laughing with delight because her family was all at home. Grandpa and some of the Uncles would either play crokinole, or exchange stories in the basement while probably having a little sip. One of Grandma's rules was no booze upstairs. She kind of ignored it downstairs. The important part was that everyone got along and the walls were always vibrating with the sound of laughter.

The Taverner family loved to tell stories. They could make the most boring situation into a hilarious story. I come by my storytelling naturally because it's in my genes. My Uncles loved to play and they seemed to have as much fun as I did with my new presents. One year, I got a hockey game and we all played with it. The basement was filled with the sounds of "He shoots, he scores!" and "When is it my turn?"

They could make a simple game so much fun.

When the call came that dinner was ready, about twenty adults gathered around the table while my cousins and I sat at the famous kids' table. Before the meal, everyone joined hands and sang grace:

> *Be present at our table Lord,*
> *Be here and everywhere adored.*
> *These mercies bless and grant that we*
> *May live in Paradise with thee.*
> *Amen.*

The table became a beehive of activity. Plates were rattling while everyone tried to get a word in edgewise. One of my favourite memories is watching Grandma taking orders for pie, while Uncle Ron was busy telling a story about a man who would always eat so- o-o-o much food. Suddenly, we heard a terrific bang. Uncle Ron's chair had collapsed completely and he was sitting on the floor. The room fell silent. Uncle Ron's head poked up over the edge of the table, he raised his hand, and said, "Skip the pie, Mother."

Roars of laughter followed.

I remember Grandpa Rebman taking everyone for a horse-drawn sleigh ride. The fun continued until it was time to walk to Grandma Rebman's, for another Rebman turkey supper, with Grandma's special carrot pudding for dessert. These dinners were always quieter than at the Taverner house, not nearly as boisterous. When the dishes were done, everyone headed to the parlour, to gather around the old pump organ, to sing hymns. Grandma and Grandpa Taverner always came up to join in the singing. Mom played the organ and everyone suggested a favourite hymn. *In the Garden* was one song that was always sung.

Sometimes when I'm working in the garden, I find myself singing the hymn and feel the memories come flooding back, dancing in my head.

Somehow, I think it is fitting to end this book with a song – a song of joy. This copy was taken from my Grandma Taverner's old hymn book. Note the copyright is dated 1912.

Acknowledgments

I would like to thank the following individuals who helped me with this book.

To those friends who took a special interest in my project and kept cheering me on: Dr. David Kent and Bill Fee (BF), Roz and Lynne Haven.

To Carol Wagg, who helped with proofreading and spent hours inserting pictures which later had to be removed before printing. She still soldiered on, helping scan the pictures, all over again.

To my sisters, Cathy Ball, Sally Bullock, Linda Boyes, Valerie Gallon, and Nancy Tost, who always kept me sane.

To Sue Robertson, my travelling buddy and inspiration. Sue sketched the lavender and herb garden pots.

To My Fish and Chip Friends, my dear friend Mary McCulley who has always been there for me, Brenda Paterson who proofread and gave publishing advice and one of my greatest fans, Diana Aspin, an author who helped proofread, made some great suggestions and inspired me to continue.

To Sue French, who read my manuscript and later, shared a moment of tears.

To Roland and Sandy Cardy, the author, who encouraged me and gave helpful suggestions along the way.

To Michael Fitzgerald, who was patient with my emails and made perfect editing suggestions, which got me on the right track.

To Ken Murray, author of *Eulogy*, who taught a writer's course in Haliburton. He helped develop my confidence. I valued his input and interest, which continued well after the course was completed.

To Ruth and Rick Gallop, the authors of the *GI Diet* books. Thank you for taking the time to read my manuscript and to give me your feedback.

To Andrea Knight, editor, who added her expertise to make my manuscript flow more smoothly.

To Ron Jacques, friend and editor, a special thank-you for bringing "new eyes" to my manuscript and helping to polish it in the final stages.

To our local Authors' Association members who gave me confidence in my work. A special thanks to Wendie Donabie, who works so hard for the organization and other author groups. She still took the time to read my manuscript to make some great suggestions.

To Yvonne Heath, who shared with me our writing journey and our passion to help others. She was writing her book *Love Your Life to Death*.

To Sandy Gohm, who lost her dear Peter and reminded me what it was like to struggle.

To my dear Aunt Eileen Taverner who I have admired my whole life. She turned ninety-years-old this year, still lives in her own home and we say good night on the phone most nights.

To my husband, Bill, who grew tired of seeing me with my head stuck at the computer and watching me tossing and turning in bed, while new passages rolled around in my mind.

To Allan Vilela, the photographer who took my author's photo during a cruise across the Atlantic. I wish Allan best wishes for his new studio in Rio de Joneiro, Brazil. He is a talented, hardworking, young photographer, who touched my heart with his kindness and sincerity.

This picture was taken in December 1997, on Bill's fiftieth birthday. We all seemed to be beaming – it's hard to believe that eight months later we would lose one of our shining lights and life as we knew it, would be gone forever. My journey was about to begin.

> *Our loved ones leave behind spaces in the*
> *world that can never be filled.*
> *But they also leave behind "love" and "light" in each of us.*
> *Sparks of "joy" and "hope" that live in our*
> *hearts and give strength to our souls.*

AUTHOR UNKNOWN

Printed in Canada